GRACE | A BIOGRAPHY
PARAMORE

BEN WELCH

BY
BEN WELCH

INDEPENDENT MUSIC PRESS

Published in 2009 by

INDEPENDENT MUSIC PRESS

Independent Music Press is an imprint of I.M. P. Publishing Limited
This Work is Copyright © I.M.P. Publishing Ltd 2009

Grace: A Biography of Paramore
by Ben Welch

British Library Cataloguing-in-Publication Data.
A catalogue for this book is available from The British Library.

ISBN 978-1-906191-16-0

Every effort has been made to contact the photographers whose
work has been used in this book - however a few were unobtainable.
The publishers would be grateful if those concerned would contact
Independent Music Press Ltd.

Cover design by Fresh Lemon
Cover photograph by Nigel Crane

Independent Music Press
P.O. Box 69,
Church Stretton, Shropshire
SY6 6WZ
Visit us on the web at:
www.impbooks.com
Fax: 01694 720049

Contents

ACKNOWLEDGEMENTS & PHOTO CREDITS

The author would like to thank the following people who interviewed exclusively for this book: Randall Thomas, Lucio Rubino, Ashley Brown, Mary Bonney, Joe Shooman. The author would also like to thank the writers and magazines whose articles are among the best and most in-depth insights into all things Paramore: 'Seeing Things', *Kerrang!*, Rae Alexander, issue 1279, September 09; 'Teen Titans', *Kerrang!*, Ian Winwood, Issue 1129, October 06; 'Teenage Rampage', *Kerrang!*, Emma Johnston, May 06; 'Loved Up', *The Big Cheese*, Jim Sharples, February 08; 'Born For This', *Alternative Press*, Steven Robertshaw, 27/5/08; 'Misery Is Their Business.... And Business Is Good', *Alternative Press*, Jonah Bayer, 10/11/07; 'You Know Nothing of The Crush', *Alternative Press*, Leslie Simon, October 09; Julia Conny, Interview for *Absolutepunk.net*, 25/05/07; Paramore Interview for *Music Scene Media*, Jesse Gonzalez and Lance Paris, 20/01/06; 'No Rest For the Virtuous', *Rock Sound*, Andrew Kelham, Issue 107 March 08; *MTV.com*, James Montgomery News articles.

Author's Dedication: My sincerest thanks to Mum, Dad and Krystal; Mart, Kaye and Dave at Independent Music Press; Ian, Ed, Chris and all the Coach House Associates; and everyone who offered their time to help with this book.

The author and publisher would like to express a special thanks to the photographers Nigel Crane, Ashley Brown and Kieran Meyn.

Photo Credits:
Nigel Crane: 6, 18, 53 (btm), 55, 60, 64, 67, 90, 93, 97, 99, 102, 107, 109, 132, 135, 136, 140, 144; Kieran Meyn: 10, 36, 37; Ashley Brown: 20, 23, 27, 32, 42, 46, 53 (top), 59(top); Karl Walter/Getty: 59(bottom), 119; Chris Gordon/Getty: 73; G. Gershoff/Getty: 79; Kevin Winter/Getty: 82; Daniel Boczarski/Getty: 86; Jeff Kravitz/Getty: 88(bottom); Lester Cohen/Getty: 114; Christopher Polk/Getty: 116; Rob Loud/Getty: 126(top); Michael Buckner/Getty: 128.

INTRODUCTION

In a rented rehearsal space in Nashville, Tennessee, Paramore are in pre-production for their third album. Their previous effort, *Riot!*, was certified platinum in the US and gold in the UK, Ireland and New Zealand. It took them on a headlining tour around the world, from the States to Canada, through Europe to Japan and back again, including stop-offs at Reading and Leeds, and the 'Give It A Name' and 'Warped' tours. It earned them a Grammy nomination, as well as the accolade of 'Best Band of 2007' from *Alternative Press*. And yet, despite all this success, Paramore are on the brink of implosion.

Constant touring has taken its toll on the band, the rigours of life on the road and absence of sufficient time-off wearing away at their long-standing friendships. Songs simply aren't coming together the way they should and as pre-production falters, the frustration is overwhelming enthusiasm. Their endlessly dynamic and charismatic front-woman Hayley Williams, who the media has often lavished with attention at the expense of her band mates, has doubts that they will even complete the record. Since the cancellation of the final leg of their European tour – a somewhat cryptic blog entry offering "internal issues" as the reason – fan forums have been awash with speculation that the end is nigh for Paramore. A small number of followers begin to point fingers at members of the band, drawing on scant personal details and rumour to substantiate their theories as to who is responsible for the friction. Despite rocketing to international stardom in adolescence – the oldest member of the band being just 24 and the youngest still in his teens – Paramore's future is looking decidedly bleak.

And yet, they will not just survive this crisis, they will conquer it, restoring their lost passion and returning with their most accomplished and deeply personal record to date. They will win critical acclaim, restore the faith of old fans and win a legion of new ones. They will embark on a sell-out arena tour and secure their seat at the summit of contemporary rock music.

Even if, just for a moment, it looked like they might not make it.

chapter 1

FRIENDS, FRICTION AND FCS

Tennessee: the fertile strip of land that borders eight other states in the south-eastern US. The land where Jack Daniels distilled his famous whisky, Patti Page danced the waltz with her darlin', and Mark Cohn walked in Memphis some fourteen years after Elvis died there. The land where one acre, according to President Andrew Jackson's wife Rachel, is worth a thousand Floridian acres. Maybe there is something in the soil, because Tennessee also gave the world Paramore: a Grammy-nominated, platinum-selling rock band adored by millions of fans around the world.

But the story really starts some three hundred miles to the south, in the old railroad town of Meridian, Mississippi. Up to the mid-1950s, Meridian had been something of an economic hub, with a network of railway lines converging within its centre, transporting vital assets such as timber throughout the US. But with the decline of rail as the principal mode of haulage in the 1950s, Meridian would find itself forced to diversify its economy, and only partially managed to traverse the many pitfalls that the rapid changes of the 20th Century presented. Throughout the 1980s the population began to slowly but steadily decrease as unemployment rates crept up. Yet despite these somewhat grim facts, Meridian was and remains a cultural hotspot in Mississippi. It boasts an impressive roster of residents who have made a name in music, as well as being the birthplace of Hartley Peavey, founder of musical equipment manufacturer Peavey Electronics. While Peavey gear is used by recording artists all over the world, from US metallers Slipknot to 1980s New Wavers Duran Duran, its headquarters still resides in Meridian.

The year is 1988. George Michael's *Faith* is flying off the shelves and into the homes of young men and women all over the country, U2 will accept a Grammy for *The Joshua Tree*, and America's previously underground urban musicians will start to find a mainstream platform with the release of NWA's

Straight Outta Compton. Just below the surface, bands like Pixies, Sonic Youth and Dinosaur Jr. are reinventing alternative rock and laying the groundwork for arguably the most important development in guitar music since punk: grunge and the rise of Nirvana. And on December 27, Joey and Christie Williams welcomed their first daughter into the world: Hayley Nichole Williams.

Details of her early years are relatively scant, but Hayley seemed to pass her first few in domestic harmony. She recalls the simple joys of childhood, like singing along to the radio, and her delight at dining with Mickey Mouse on a trip to Disney World aged four or five ("that was pretty rad!"). Her mother was a fan of jazz and pop and a keen dancer, who exposed Hayley to a varied selection of music. Her father, on the other hand, was more interested in classic rock and the testosterone-fuelled hard riffery of bands like Aerosmith and Van Halen. They came to an agreement on their love of Motown, soul and funk, however; so from an early age, Hayley was listening to a wide range of musical styles, coming to understand the beauty of melody, the importance of rhythm, and the power of unbridled rock.

But Hayley's childhood was not without its drama, and aged just eight, the serenity of her home life was shattered as her parent's relationship fell apart. It was an experience that unsurprisingly seems to have left a profound impression on her, with many of the lyrics she would later come to write drawing on this deep well of pain. At the time she could only despair and attempt to block out the distress: "I remember actually walking out the door with my mom that night and standing in between my parents and screaming, 'Shut up! Shut up! Shut up!'" she recalled in an interview with *Alternative Press* in 2008. Their parents went on to seek a divorce, which was becoming increasingly prevalent in the 1980s: in 1985, South Dakota was the last US State to legalise no-fault divorces, whereby neither party had to prove that their spouse was guilty of a crime or sin in order to legally end the marriage. But despite this, divorce remained a taboo in the deeply religious southern states of America. The Williams family were practising Southern Baptists, a denomination of Christianity often regarded as somewhat conservative, which upholds and encourages traditional gender roles. A 1998 addition to the Baptist Faith and Message, a document which outlines the Baptist's views and readings of the Bible, states: "A wife is to submit herself graciously to the servant leadership of her husband even as the church willingly submits to the headship of Christ." With statements like this in mind, it is unsurprising that some Baptists took a dim view of divorce, a fact that would later cause more disruption in the William's household.

After the divorce, both of her parents would remarry, but their relationship with one another would continue to deteriorate. The main source of tension, according to Hayley, was her new stepfather who she has since been openly critical of in the press, saying he was "very controlling". One day, Hayley came home from school to find her mother's car packed with all their possessions. They got in and drove to a nearby trailer park, where they would live for six months, before moving to Nashville, Tennessee, to start a new life.

But the second divorce that Hayley was expecting and hoping for didn't come. Instead, feeling pressure from some elements of the Southern Baptist community, Hayley's mother Christie decided to return to Meridian and make a go of her second marriage. Hayley had just begun to settle into life in Nashville, and she remembers receiving the news as "the worst day of my life." They returned to Meridian, but not for a long time: Hayley is unsure of exactly what happened, but she hints at some upsetting event that drove her mother away from her stepfather once and for all. "I still don't know what … because she kept it hidden from me," she said in *Kerrang!*. "I don't think I'll ever be able to ask her." What she does know is that her mother took her away from Meridian once and for all, to start again in Franklin, Tennessee. But despite the indelible impression that this traumatic experience has left on her, Hayley is able to see that sometimes with trials come blessings too – like her two younger half-sisters – and that painful experiences also bestow wisdom and resilience: "I'm glad I went through that stuff because the opposite of love was demonstrated to me through my mom and stepdad's relationship," she continued. "I feel like it really has shaped me and taught me a lot about how the notion of love can be misconstrued and twisted." It is a notion she would return to again and again in her more reflective moments on record.

And so Hayley found herself moving to another state, but it was in Tennessee that she would truly find her place. It was the late 1990s, a decade launched by the explosion of grunge and the Seattle sound some 2,500 miles northwest. Nirvana and contemporaries like Soundgarden, Pearl Jam and Mudhoney had initially blasted away the last bloated remnants of 1980s

Hayley in her mid-teens.

cock rock with their agricultural mix of hardcore punk and alternative rock. But since legendary Nirvana frontman Kurt Cobain had died in the spring of 1994 from a self-inflicted shotgun wound to the head, the 'movement' had began to lose momentum, and mainstream pop had restated its claim on the airwaves. Surprisingly, it was initially this pop revival rather than its grunge forerunner that the young Hayley Williams was drawn to.

For Hayley, it was hyper-preened boy band *NSYNC that had really captured her heart, whose lead singer Justin Timberlake was himself a native of Memphis. Two hundred miles north-east in Nashville – where Hayley had lived for a few months with her mother before briefly returning to Meridian – the town's sidewalks also throbbed to the beat of music. Nashville was and remains a mecca for music fans the world over. In the 1950s a multi-million dollar country music industry was centred in Nashville, and since the 1970s to the present day it has hosted the Country Music Association Festival.

Hayley and her mother landed in Franklin, itself a small town of just over forty thousand inhabitants, south of Nashville and almost due east of Memphis. It has a number of famous residents, particularly musicians, to its name – actress Ashley Judd and singer Alison Krauss among them – but for the most part, Franklin is a typical, pleasant, well-to-do southern town. And while it might be a million miles from the likes of New York, Chicago or San Francisco in both size and musical activity, it was and remains home to Paramore, and dear to all of them. As Hayley stated simply in 2006: "I like Franklin. It's calm and friendly. I feel safe here." She began attending middle school in Leiper's Fork, a tiny village in Williamson County, around ten miles west of Franklin. Her mother was teaching in another local school and was acutely aware that Hayley was struggling to make new friends. Since the age of eleven, Hayley had discovered a passion and talent for singing, and was taking every opportunity to exercise it at school and church. So seeing flyers posted all over her school offering auditions to be the singer in a local band, Christie suggested her daughter try out. Hayley still remembers her rallying enthusiasm: "You love singing, and you like this kind of music, so let's do this, let's try to make you some friends!" The band was called The Factory, and played mainly funk and soul covers – "party music," as Hayley put it – songs by the likes of Michael Macdonald, Stevie Wonder, Jamiroquai and Aretha Franklin. They had enjoyed relative success, too: getting to visit other schools after impressing the tutors at their own, and eventually even playing shows out of town. But the singer of the band had unexpectedly left, so wanting to keep their successful run going, they'd posted the audition adverts around schools in the area. The audition took place in the drummer's house, where the band had set up a microphone alongside their equipment for Hayley to demonstrate her skills. Despite being incredibly nervous, she won over her potential band mates and was immediately accepted into the fold. In Paramore's history, it was a vital development, though none could have possibly known it – because the bassist was one Jeremy Davis Clayton.

Born on February 8, 1985, in Little Rock, Arkansas, Jeremy is three years Hayley's senior, and at the time of the audition, around fourteen. The son of a children's pastor, he had always wanted to play the guitar like his dad. Instead he was encouraged to try the bass, with the incentive that he could accompany his father when he sang in church. He was given a starter bass guitar and from there his passion was ignited, and he played in church with his father for a year. However, it was the school in Leiper's Fork that really developed his fledgling musical ambitions, through a program called 'Kids On Stage'. "It's this really tiny town in the middle of nowhere, but they have one of the best music programs in the country," Davis said. He even got the chance to take a class called 'Rock Band' – which sounds like something Jack Black should be teaching in a major Hollywood picture – where to get good grades, he had to cover rock songs. Jeremy states that the school program had a huge effect on him, and that he believes it got him to where he is today: "That's where I learned to play guitar and where I started playing in [The Factory] – and that's where I met Hayley." The Factory began rehearsing together and was soon playing shows at a local venue called Green's Grocery. Hayley and Jeremy had taken their first steps towards a long stretch of collaboration that would bring huge success to both of them.

But for the time being, Hayley had bigger issues on her mind. She was struggling to settle in the new school, despite the friendship and distraction The Factory offered her. She remembers it now as a "terrible experience," and so decided to leave. The decision was made that she be home-schooled, attending a once-a-week supplemental tutoring program to direct her studies. And it was here that Paramore would truly begin to take shape.

Hayley was still performing with The Factory and travelling around local Franklin venues. One day, whilst attending the once-a-week appointment with her tutors, she remembers a "little fat kid" – her own words – excitedly running up and telling her about a band he was in with his brother. The little fat kid in question was Zachary Wayne Farro, brother of Josh, the soon-to-be rhythmic powerhouse of Paramore.

Zac and his brother were born in Vorhees, New Jersey; Josh on 29 September, 1987, and Zac on June 4, 1990, making him around eleven at the time of his first meeting with Hayley. He had only owned his drum kit for less than a year, but his passion had first been ignited at the age of nine in a school program ingeniously entitled 'Bach to Rock.' Aimed at encouraging students to take up an instrument, the teacher had brought in a red drum kit to show the class. He asked which of the students would like to come and try out the drums, and it was Zac that decided to raise his hand and brave the stares of his classmates. The teacher demonstrated a simple beat and Zac followed suit. From there he was hooked. He went home and set up the "typical pots and pans drum set" before graduating to a "bean bag and pillow." As soon as he reached his eleventh birthday and was given a drum kit as a gift, him and his brother Josh began jamming together.

At this time Josh had already begun his own development as a musician. Randall Thomas is a friend who attended school with both of the brothers, and offers a real insight into the formative years of both the Farros and Paramore. Whilst Randall, Josh and Zac all went to the same one-day-a-week supplemental program as Hayley, they also attended Franklin Classical School, or FCS, for four days a week. Randall was already aware of Josh through the friendship of their mothers, as he told the author for this book: "I think I met Josh a long time ago; before we were actually friends our mothers worked together at one of the YMCA's here. So I probably met him for the first time when I was around seven or eight." But it was FCS that would truly cement their friendship, which has lasted to this day. "Later on we started going to high school together, about 6th grade... that's about 12 or 13," he revealed. "Me and Josh were in the same grade so we became, pretty much, best friends. So when I started hanging out a lot with Josh, I started hanging out with Zac also."

Throughout his childhood Josh had been enjoying varied, if somewhat dubious musical delights: from velvet-voiced North Carolina folkster James Taylor to Merseyside carrot-top crooner Rick Astley. But Randall remembers their experience at FCS as being particularly positive: "FCS had a lot of really artistic kids and a lot of raw talent there," he said. "I think that the school helped, I know at least it helped me, to start thinking on my own and not just taking information at face value – really looking into things and questioning things. It was really good for kind of... making individuals." It was in this relaxed atmosphere of free-thinking that Randall and Josh would begin to indulge their passion for music together.

In the late 1990s Josh had found the likes of Self and Failure. Self, a Tennessee act themselves, were and still are fronted by multi-instrumentalist

Matt Mahaffey, and their 1995 debut *Subliminal Plastic Motives* had won plaudits for its experimental and wide-ranging alt-rock. Likewise, Failure were often lumped in with the likes of Soundgarden and Nirvana in the early 1990s, but their expansive and highly textured sound had set them apart. With his newly refined penchant for underground alternative rock, Josh began to take an interest in learning the guitar – though Randall remembers that he and Josh also had a passion for something altogether more British than 1990s alt-rock. "At FCS there was like a small group of cool people, and we ended up listening to a lot of music that the kids of FCS listened to, a lot of Muse and Radiohead." It was particularly the epic, intricate rock stylings of Muse that Randall and Josh would first try to emulate when they began playing music together.

But for the time being, Josh still had to learn to play, and he did so on what he calls a "really old, crappy acoustic." Self-taught, he would listen to CDs over and over, rewinding individual parts until he had got it down pat (legendary guitarists such as Jimi Hendrix, Eric Clapton and Guns N' Roses' Slash are all similarly self-taught). One of the first albums to truly capture his imagination was *Morning View,* the third studio album of American rock group Incubus, released in 2001. *Morning View* was Incubus's first release to truly channel the easy-living spirit of the West Coast, and guitarist Mike Einziger's combination of strong alternative rock riffs and more ambient, psychedelic lead work won him many plaudits. It's not surprising, then, that Josh recalls sitting down night after night teaching himself every song on the album. Randall remembers that his progress on the guitar was nothing short of astonishing: "I actually started playing guitar and Josh was the singer. And then a couple of years later we kind of switched places. He's pretty much all self-taught. He just practised every day for so long, it really didn't take him that long at all. I'd been playing guitar years before him and he just bypassed me. I found out I could sing, so… we just kind of, switched places." And Randall is under no illusions as to what aspect of Josh's character allowed him to progress so rapidly on the guitar. "Josh has always been a really driven person, and did everything that he wanted to do one hundred and twenty percent," he revealed. "He's probably the most focused person I've ever met."

At the time Zac first introduced himself to Hayley, him and his brother had been playing together for a while in their parent's house, covering everything from geek-rockers Weezer to pop-punkers Sum 41 and, of course,

Josh's beloved Incubus. The brothers and Randall would later also form a band called Seraphim, as an outlet for their musical ambitions. Randall loved writing with Josh, who he says is one of the easiest people he's ever written with: "I don't know if it's just because we've written together for so long that we have such great chemistry, or he just writes like that with everybody," he remarked. They would meet up in a spare room in the Farro house – a kind of "bonus room," as Randall puts it – that the brothers had once shared. There they would write material and jam, but whenever Randall wasn't there, the brothers would be in that room anyway. "We had most of our equipment set up at their house so when they weren't practising with me, they were writing together," Randall explained. "Josh would come up with something and want to hear it with a drum beat."

Despite having only been playing the drums for a short time, Zac's progress had also been incredibly rapid, much like his brother. "In the beginning, Zac was still a little bit timid about playing," Randall says, "and Josh would sort of throw out ideas and Zac would take them and build on them and even make them better. Ever since he started, he just amazes us. By the time he was fourteen he was already pretty much a professional." The noise coming from the "bonus room" in the Farro house must have been as frequent as it was deafening, but as far as Randall remembers, the Farro elders never offered anything but encouragement to the budding musicians. "They never yelled at us for making too much noise or anything like that. They would flip us a good word and tell us that we sounded good or whatever. I'm not sure if they were particularly grateful for us making all the noise in their house, but they never told us not to do it."

chapter 2

FALLING INTO PLACE

At the same time as writing and rehearsing with Randall Thomas, the Farro brothers continued to write their own fledgling material. They rehearsed every Thursday after their schooling and since Zac had first approached Hayley, they began inviting her to sit in – they had an idea that she might be into the same kind of music as them, and had a mind to ask her to become their singer. She was already known in school for her vocal talent, as Randall remembers: "Her voice was pretty much the same as it is now. She showed up at the school and when we heard her sing, everybody was just so amazed because there was this tiny little girl and this giant voice coming out of her." The Farro brothers wanted Hayley's involvement in their music and would in turn play a part in turning her into the alternative icon she is today. Their friendship was, according to Hayley, "really built on mix CDs," and they would share new discoveries and old passions with one another – trading songs by bands such as Failure, Thursday, Death Cab for Cutie, Jimmy Eat World and perhaps most importantly, Sunny Day Real Estate. It was unusual to find someone with a similar taste in music, Hayley noted, as the scene around Nashville was so predominantly based on country ("we do not listen to country, even though we are from Tennessee," she would later quip to *Absolutepunk.net*).

Many of the groups on these mix tapes have their roots in the 1980s, and particularly the hardcore punk scene – bands like Black Flag, Bad Brains and Minor Threat. In contrast to what is typically thought of as 'emo' today, the early hardcore scene was often openly political, socially conscious and aggressive in nature. But towards the mid-1980s, Minor Threat fan Guy Picciotto would reject the outward-looking attitude and turn the gaze inward, forming his own band Rites Of Spring, with personal, confessional lyrics and notoriously emotionally intense live shows (Minor Threat frontman Ian MacKaye would later go on to form legendary post-hardcore band Fugazi alongside Picciotto). It is with the seminal Rites Of Spring, however, that perhaps the term 'emo' first developed; author Andy Greenwald, in his book *Nothing Feels Good: Punk Rock, Teenagers and Emo*, writes: "If Minor Threat was hardcore, then Rites Of Spring, with its altered focus, was emotional hardcore or emocore." By the end of the 1980s, the vast majority of the bands involved in the formative scene had dissolved, but the 1990s would bring with it emo's resurrection.

Sunny Day Real Estate were in part responsible for this. Their debut album *Diary* was released in 1994, a month after Kurt Cobain's suicide signalled the death-throes of the grunge explosion that had hijacked the mainstream channels. Like Nirvana, they were from Seattle and signed to Sub Pop Records, but they strove for a more expansive, epic sound. *Diary* combined buzz-saw guitars and rapid-fire hard rock drumming with lead singer Jeremy Enigk's high-pitched, fragile vocals – all with a typically Sub Pop lo-fi sound. Fraught and frenetic tracks like 'Seven' and 'Round' sit alongside slow-burners like 'Song About An Angel' and 'Grendel', showcasing the band's grasp of their hardcore roots and more melodic, epic intent. Enigk would also win plaudits for his oblique, confessional lyrics.

Sunny Day Real Estate would split for the first time in 1995, prior to the release of their second album, posthumously titled *LP2*. Bassist Nate Mendel and drummer William Goldsmith would join the new project of ex-Nirvana drummer Dave Grohl, the Foo Fighters (Nate is now the longest standing member after Grohl himself). SDRE would regroup for the first time in 1997, without Mendel, to record their third album *How It Feels To Be Something On*, and follow this up in 2000 with *The Rising Tide*. While not greeted with the same buzz as their debut *Diary*, and perhaps not as immediate, *The Rising Tide* is probably their masterpiece. Despite Sunny Day Real Estate's unsettled history and failure to truly break into the mainstream – they would never even tour overseas – their influence has bled into the records of countless bands since. Paramore would frequently cite them as a major influence, and it's easy to see why: personal lyrics woven into expressive, stirring melodies, framed by a sturdy rhythm section and simple, direct guitar work. Paramore would even go on to cover 'Faces In Disguise' from *The Rising Tide*, a song Hayley Williams says she could listen to over and over on repeat.

Also regulars alongside SDRE on Zac and Josh's celebrated mix tapes were Jimmy Eat World from Mesa, Arizona, who had probably asserted themselves as the heirs to Sunny Day's throne, with their shamelessly catchy and emotive pop-rock. They emerged alongside other bands from the mid-western United States, like Mineral and The Promise Ring of Colorado. While their second album *Clarity* had drawn plenty of acclaim, it was their third *Bleed American* (later re-issued as *Jimmy Eat World* in the wake of the September 11, 2001 attacks) that turned them into international contenders. It would ultimately be certified platinum, with second single 'The Middle' getting significant play on MTV.

Alongside Jimmy's crafted pop stylings, Hayley was also being offered something a little harder on these mix tapes. Thursday had formed in the late 1990s in New Jersey, and would become one of the most successful 'post-hardcore' bands, taking their cues from hardcore and emocore but eschewing straightforward arrangements in favour of a more experimental, challenging sound. In light of the screamed vocals that Thursday and contemporaries like

Farro brothers Zac and Josh.

Glassjaw and Thrice had adopted, lending the bands a certain emotional intensity and fierceness to their sound, the term 'screamo' was thrown about (though this label can actually be traced back to many post-hardcore bands from the 1990s). Heavy, dissonant and eclectic, Thursday were perhaps the first band that Hayley was drawn to that fell on the other side of the invisible line between what might broadly be called 'pop' and heavier music. It was a penchant that she would develop and indulge, alongside her band mates, who now frequently reference bone-shakingly noisy hardcore bands like Norma Jean and The Chariot.

Of course, any brief potted history of a scene such as this is bound to omit and simplify – no musical movement is a simple linear development from one band to the next – but this does serve to illustrate some of the key players in alternative music of the late 1990s and early 2000s, and particularly those that have had a clear influence on Paramore's sound. The point is that Zac and Josh along with their mix tapes had opened a Pandora's box of musical possibilities. For the first time since her trials at school in Leiper's Fork, Hayley had found like-minded individuals to bind with, and as is the case for many teenagers, the common ground was music: "A whole new side of music," as Hayley puts it, and one that would ultimately take her and her new friends to global success.

With Hayley regularly sitting in on Josh and Zac's garage band sessions, she inevitably began singing and writing with the brothers. However she began to find that singing with such full-blooded force was straining her voice, so she decided to look for some tuition. She sought out one Brett Manning of Nashville, who began training her. Manning has since become one of the most esteemed vocal coaches in America, with endorsements from teen pop sensations Miley Cyrus and Taylor Swift, and Australian country megastar Keith Urban. The chemistry between Hayley and her new tutor was immediate and she credits Manning with developing her voice to the distinctive and powerful instrument it is today, saying that he took her voice to a "whole new level." Hayley continues to visit Manning to this day, claiming that she would rather fly him to her than visit another coach.

With Hayley's voice becoming stronger with each lesson, the trio decided it was time to fill out their fledgling musical project with other members. When it came to looking for a bass player, the choice was obvious; on Hayley's recommendation they asked Jeremy Davis, from The Factory. She

Founder member Jeremy Davis.

convinced the brothers by telling them he had a real natural musicality and could play pretty much anything on the bass; they agreed to the idea and so she gave him a call. According to Jeremy, he had agreed to come and meet her new band mates before she could even get the words out to ask him, yet it nearly never happened. A get-together was arranged for Josh and Zac to meet Davis, but first impressions were not necessarily ideal. Jeremy remembers pulling into Starbucks car park and seeing the pubescent Zac run up and jump in. Five years his senior, Jeremy's first thought was "This is not going to work because this kid is way too young." But if Paramore have proved one thing, it's that age is not necessarily an obstacle to success. From the very first rehearsal that day, Jeremy felt a synergy and knew that the four of them were on to something.

The line-up completed, they started throwing about ideas and suggestions for a name. A friend and previous collaborator's mother had the maiden name Paramore, and the band immediately liked the way it sounded (sketchy rumours suggest they may have used the name before, on a fledgling musical project that never got off the ground, but the exact details of members and the veracity of this theory is unclear). Its meaning of 'secret lover' was also an appealingly romantic inference.

At the time that Paramore were forming, Josh and Zac were still jamming with school friend Randall Thomas in their other band Seraphim. They had recorded a couple of demos in Randall's dad's recording studio (Randall comes from a family of musicians), a stripped-out barn called The Radio Ranch Recording Studio (these early recordings are available to hear on Randall Thomas' MySpace, at *myspace.com/randallthomas*). Even in these initial recordings, you can hear some of the germinal aspects of Josh and Zac's playing. "If you go back and listen to the Seraphim stuff," says Randall, "even back then Josh was writing powerful riffs. I guess that it comes from not taking any lessons or anything. I guess he just developed his own style."

Under the Seraphim monicker, Randall and Josh had recruited a bassist and another guitarist and played a few shows, including one at the Franklin Mercantile, a deli which put on the occasional gig at the weekend. One short-term participant in Seraphim as a guitarist was also a certain Taylor York, a fellow pupil at FCS (who would later reappear in Paramore's history as the third guitar player to stand alongside Josh).

In the meantime, Paramore were also developing, helped by various members of the band performing individually at school talent shows. They soon enlisted Hayley's next-door neighbour, Jason Bynum, to fill out their sound as a second guitarist. The first song they wrote together as a band was 'Conspiracy', which would later appear on their debut album. Growing in confidence, they began looking for gigs outside of school, but Randall remembers that they did not rush into playing every show they were offered. "They mostly kept underground," he says. "They just practised a ton and then every once in a while they'd go and play a show that everybody would show up to." The first real show that Paramore would ever play was supporting Copeland, at the popular Nashville venue The End. Copeland, a Floridian band, had formed in 2000 and signed to Tooth & Nail Records, a Seattle based label that predominantly signs Christian bands. Copeland had a big following in Franklin, particularly amongst Paramore's peer group, and were in fact the first band that Hayley ever paid to see with her friends. Every time they would play Nashville, Hayley said that, "all of Franklin was there." In fact, she claims that half of the audience on the night of her band's debut gig were friends who had planned to attend before they even knew Paramore were playing. She recalls the pre-show excitement at opening for one of their favourite bands: Paramore collected in a huddle and nervously chattering, with the reality of what they were about to do slowly dawning on them. Randall Thomas was also present at the gig, and recalls a similar sense of excited anticipation in the audience. "If I remember correctly, everyone was really, really excited to see Paramore," he said. "I'm sure that was the first time for a lot of people to see them all together, but at the school everybody had pretty much heard Hayley sing and Josh was always playing guitar. So they had heard them individually but not the whole band together. And at that point, Copeland and [other support band] Lovedrug were also pretty big bands that everybody was listening to. So the whole event was really exciting for everybody."

Because of their understandable excitement, Paramore played all of their songs too fast – "we sounded like chipmunks," Hayley remembers – but the experience was nothing short of eye-opening all the same. The fledgling band played many tracks which would later appear on their debut album, and the night was the first time that Hayley truly started to believe that they could make a serious go of Paramore. It had always been a dream but playing a show had made it a reality – albeit a distant one. "As soon as we started and realised how much we all loved it and shared a passion for it," she says, they knew that there was "nothing else for us, it has to work out." Randall also remembers the twenty-five minute set just as fondly. "It was a really cool show. It was a *really* great show," he disclosed.

It wasn't just personal ambitions that the band was helping to nurture, either. It also was also having a positive effect on Hayley's home life. Her parents had struggled to remain cordial after her mother's tumultuous relationship with her second husband. But as the band began to take their

Early live shot with Jason Bynum.

new venture more seriously, her parents agreed that to make things as easy as possible for their daughter, they should settle their differences. For the first year of Paramore's life, Hayley's parents were regularly taking their turn to ferry the band and their gear around. "If they were fighting, it would have been hell," Hayley observes.

The band continued gigging for the following year in Nashville alone, and to all intents and purposes were still a parochial act known only by locals – although in 2004 they had travelled further afield to Pennsylvania for a slot at the Purple Door Christian festival.

They had also drawn enough attention to attract a management deal with a well-respected team from Orlando, who knew people on the influential independent label Fueled By Ramen. Founded in 1996 by alternative music Svengali John Janick, Fueled By Ramen released Jimmy Eat World's breakthrough, self-titled EP in 1998 and would go on to sign the likes of Fall Out Boy and Panic! At The Disco early in their careers. By 2004, Fueled By Ramen was a force to be reckoned with.

John Janick had got hold of some of Paramore's demos and was impressed. By a lucky coincidence, Paramore had recently entered and won a Battle of the Bands competition to perform at the Orlando stop of the very first 'Taste of Chaos' tour, on February 18, 2005, where John Janick was in attendance. After seeing the band in the flesh, his interest was well and truly piqued, but he was not yet completely sold – he wanted to see the band one more time, in a more intimate location.

A private show was therefore set up for the key players at Fueled By Ramen, in an abandoned day-care centre next to Paramore's practice space, where they were asked to play both electric and acoustic sets. After the showcase, and given the opportunity to meet many of Fueled By Ramen's staff, the band was sure that that they had found the label for them. It wasn't a difficult decision, either: when asked what attracted Paramore to Fueled By Ramen, Hayley simply stated in *Music Scene Media* that, "because everyone there loves music and it helps us be a better band." In April of 2005 they travelled to the label's office in Tampa, Florida, and were offered a record deal. It was a day Hayley rates as twelve on a one-to-ten scale of excitement. John Janick was not reserved in his praise of the band, either. "I seldom find a band I feel compelled to work with after just one encounter," he said on *music365.com*, adding that he knew he had to put out the Paramore record after meeting them. "Their talent, sincerity and dedication exceeds that of many bands."

Hayley was aged just sixteen, still eight months away from her seventeenth birthday; Jeremy, the band's elder statesman, was still a fresh-faced eighteen; and Zac, the baby of the band, was only fourteen years old. And yet, almost suddenly the members found themselves contracted as professional musicians. Leaving behind what schooling they had left to complete, they began preparing to relocate to Orlando and record their debut album.

But it would not be the straightforward line to success that all new bands dream of. The first in a series of major trials was about to shake Paramore to its foundations.

chapter 3

DOUBTS AND DEBUTS

Paramore moved up to Orlando to begin writing for their debut release. They felt that they needed to get away from the enjoyable distractions that home life presented, and throw themselves fully into honing their sound for their first assault on the mainstream. Josh had graduated from school just in time to begin recording the album, but Hayley, one year his junior, would finish after the completion of the album via online courses and workbooks. Zac, they joked, "will never do it."

James Paul Wisner and Mike Green, both hook-ups from Fueled By Ramen, were to take on the producer role. Paramore were huge fans of all of Wisner's work: he had been the man behind the desk on Further Seems Forever's *The Moon Is Down*, from 2001, an influential release in the new Millennium emo explosion. He would later work again with Further Seems Forever's vocalist, Chris Carrabba, on his new acoustic project Dashboard Confessional – one of the most recognisable and successful 'emo' bands. Chris Carrabba's breathy, high-pitched voice would be the blueprint for many singers that followed in his wake. Wisner had also produced Floridian metalcore band Underoath on a number of occasions, a band whom Paramore would frequently cite as one of their all-time favourites. Wisner's last project for Fueled By Ramen had been *Almost Here*, the debut album by The Academy Is…, the singles of which had received heavy airplay on MTV, making Wisner hot property as a producer of melodic rock acts. Mike Green was brought in on John Janick's suggestion. He had previously worked a lot with US punk label Epitaph, home to long-standing punkers Bad Religion, but was keen to get involved when approached by Janick. "The first thing," he explained to *Absolutepunk.net*, "is that I need to hear the band in order to determine if the project makes sense for me."

Paramore approached writing the album in the same manner that they had written since they first started. Josh acts as the "musical brains" as Hayley puts it, coming up with riffs and chord progressions as the starting point of a song. This would usually be on an acoustic guitar, a habit Josh had picked up from his days learning the instrument playing along to CDs. Typically he would then take this idea of a song to Hayley, who would begin to hum melodies and start her own creative process. Once the pair had come to some agreement on a basic structure, it would be played to the rest of the band to jam with, expand, alter and amend as they see fit. It is at this point, with a basic sense of melody in place, that Hayley begins to think of lyrics.

The lyrical process is an isolated one for Hayley. She withdraws herself from the rest of the band, drawing on the personal experiences that the music calls to mind for her. It is a process she compares to writing a diary — by which she surely means the outpouring of feelings and sensations that the noise of everyday life would usually drown out. But of course, even the most personal and confessional piece of writing must have some artifice imposed on it if it is going to work as a song. After all, if every songwriter simply transposed lyrics from his or her diary, no song would be under ten minutes long. This dichotomy is even more pronounced in acts that strive to write very emotive, cathartic lyrics, which also fit within the fairly rigid confines of a catchy melody. Hayley is well aware of this, but dismissive of any claims that Paramore's pop streak lessens the effect of her writing: "Some may say that the lyrics are pop due to the fact I use rhyme schemes, but I don't care."

From here, with a basic verse and chorus worked out, the whole band get together and take the song into the practice room, roughly half complete, and refine it until it is ready to take to the studio. It is this part of the process that Mike Green sees as particularly important in helping the band reach their full potential and making a great album. He states that a band must be ready to enter the studio when the time comes, and that the best way to ensure this is through pre-production — essentially, the pre-recording rehearsals. At this stage Green likes to start "with just acoustic guitars and vocals to really hear the essence of the songs," before getting the whole band involved to make sure they are "nailing the songs." In a post-Pro Tools world where almost any aspect of a performance can be digitally altered and tweaked to the point of perfection, Green has a refreshingly no-nonsense view on recording bands. As he says, "You could be the best producer/engineer in the world, but if you're in the room with shit talent,

i.e. bad musicians, then the end product will be crap."

Green couldn't really have asked for a higher potential for talent: a precociously promising young band, still all in their teens, with pre-production well underway on a very encouraging debut album. But Paramore's hopes were about to take a serious dent. Unbeknown to them, one of their number was in the middle of a personal crisis that would drive him out of the band.

Perhaps surprisingly it was the eldest member of the band, Jeremy Davis, who was most unsettled with the new direction that the band had taken their lives in. The exact details leading up to his departure are fairly thin on the ground, but some reports claim he was unsure that the band was really what he wanted to do with his life. The news came as a bombshell to his band mates and long-standing friends; he bought a plane ticket back to Tennessee just two weeks after moving down to Orlando, then took the band round the back of the rehearsal space and, with one hour to spare before he was due to leave, broke the news that he was leaving Paramore and going home. It was news that, according to Hayley, "just ripped us apart." "I still remember when I first told 'em," Jeremy would later recall. "Josh took off like 'Urgh!', he was so pissed. I was like, 'Ah!' It was the saddest thing ever."

Jeremy has since told *Alternative Press* that as early as the plane journey home he feared he may have made a big mistake. But despite the departure of such a key member at such a crucial time in the band's development, Paramore were up against a tight recording schedule followed by imminent touring responsibilities: they had no choice but to continue on as a four-piece. They decided to stick to the original schedule and head into the studio as planned, using session musicians to fill in for the now vacant spot of bass player. Throwing themselves into the recording with absolute conviction, the debut album was somehow completed in a matter of weeks. Zac even managed to complete the vast majority of his drum tracks in one day – a session Hayley remembers as "fun to watch." Green and Wisner still really stretched them as musicians to get the best result possible for the record, despite the difficult circumstances.

With Jeremy absent, the band called in one Lucio Rubino, a singer-songwriter and front-man of StorySide:B, a native of Saint Augustine, Florida (he is also a sought-after producer). Lucio was brought into the project by one of Paramore's managers, Mark Mercado, as he explained to the author: "I met Paramore through their management at the time which was my management as well… they asked me, they said, 'There's this really cool young band and their bass player just quit.' I had played some gigs with their manager, Mark, who was a good drummer and he'd hired me for some fun gigs in Orlando so he knew I could play, and he asked me to do it." He had already heard Paramore on a bootlegged acoustic demo of 'Hallelujah' (which would show up in a different form on second album *Riot!*), and states that he was blown away on hearing Hayley's voice for the first time.

Lucio first met the band at the studio of James Paul Wisner in St. Cloud, Florida, and three tracks were duly completed there. They clearly liked what he had done, as they asked him back to The Fort in Orlando, to finish the remaining songs for the album with Mike Green. "It was a really great experience," Lucio said. "I really fell in love with the music and… the producer, Mike Green was a really awesome guy… so it was a really fun experience." To record the bass lines [all except one], all Lucio usually had to work with were the guitar and drum tracks. This was not a difficult task because of the quality of the music, as Lucio explains: "I had a lot of fun with it… I did the majority of it in one day. I had heard the songs before so it was just like a really long day, I did seven songs in about maybe nine hours… it was fun though, 'cos this is what I do, I love playing bass and it was great music." And while Lucio states that he was impressed with the whole band, who "even at that young age were far beyond their years," two particular members of the band stood out for him. The first was Zac, who he got the chance to see record some tracks for the album. "What a great drummer," he enthused. "I mean, at fourteen he really came up with parts that were just… really cool. Not just stupid meat and potatoes – not that there's anything wrong with meat and potatoes. But he just came up with parts that really gave integrity to the music. It was really refreshing to play along with cool tracks. It allowed me to be more creative in the music." The second, of course, was Hayley, who Lucio says has "an amazing voice. Hayley, with her voice, I mean… she nailed it. All of them were really great musicians, but Hayley is just, she's spot on, man. She doesn't have to do take after take after take, she nails it." Lucio also explained that her instinct as a musician made her popular with the producers she worked with. "If you asked her to do something different she does it right away, she's got a great intuition. She's got such a great voice it doesn't need too much tweaking."

Lucio also got the chance to hang out with the band during down-time, and as he was older than them, found himself lending a sympathetic ear. "I hung out with them, and they confided in me a lot 'cos I was a little bit older. I took them out a couple of times 'cos they were really young at the time. So I took them downtown with me and they were really excited to get out, you know. They were kind of having some issues and worrying, 'cos it was all beginning for them. I'm not sure that they knew it would blew up as much as it has, but I know that they were just really excited about it. It was just a good feeling because it was great music, and everyone involved was really great." But despite their obvious excitement, he revealed that the atmosphere in the studio was "very chilled. It was very calm." A crucial element of their success, he believes, was their willingness to learn – an eagerness to improve that has no doubt driven them to where they are today. "They were very excited, very green, *per se*... but they were mature and what they lacked in experience, they made up by asking good questions."

The album was entitled *All We Know Is Falling*, a reference to the devastating effect that Jeremy's departure had on the band, and also a nod to the album's impassioned opener 'All We Know'. And it's some opener: a statement of intent for the album, the punchy, jagged guitar lines of the verse flowing into a soaring chorus, it is a plain-spoken expression of the effect that Jeremy's departure had on the band. At just over three minutes long, it crashes in as quickly as it ends, every inch dripping with irresistible melody. The guitar playing is taut and direct, and Zac's drumming, as it proves to be throughout the album, is air-tight and dynamic. But it is Hayley's vocal that really steals the show on 'All We Know'. High pitched almost to the extent of sounding strained, it shows an undeniable musicality and control, but with a real bite and edge – it doesn't have to wrestle with Josh and Jason's guitar lines, it soars above them. There's no particularly taxing metaphor lyrically, either, as she clearly speaks of the heartbreak of Jeremy leaving the band but also their resolve to continue on undaunted despite the trial. It's a straightforwardness that adds to the genuine sense of anguish in the song, and one Hayley is happy to note: "The song 'All We Know' is about Jeremy leaving us and how we couldn't understand it, and we couldn't grasp it," she said. "It wasn't really real to us. And it's almost like a letter to him saying 'I'll never forget you.'" The song was written just two days after Jeremy first told Paramore he was leaving Orlando and returning home, so the pain expressed in the song is real and very palpable. The plaintive breakdown crashes into an an-off kilter middle-eight, hinting at a desire to get a little more noisy than they ever quite manage. But as a slice of angsty, driven pop rock, it is a startling opener.

From here the album allows more melodic, pop influences to come through. The fitful opening riff of 'Pressure', the album's second track, reminds the listener of Jimmy Eat World's *Bleed American* album. The two guitar lines merge together perfectly, and once again Zac's drumming crashes in with the kind of purpose you would never expect from a fourteen-year-old player. Things calm down for the verse, with its pop-punk palm-muted guitar and choppy rhythms, but the bridge opens out, an unobtrusive organ line adding to the sense of building momentum as an almighty drum fill ushers in the chorus. Once again, it's a massive, anthemic affair, Hayley reaching into her upper register as a razor-sharp guitar lick cuts through the wall of sound. The whole song rolls on with a kind of overwhelming impetus, every subsequent section seemingly more hook-laden than the last, as Hayley sings of the drama and distress of adult relationships.

'Emergency' opens with a guitar line as clean and neat as cut glass, but soon evolves out into another full-blooded emotional rock number. The two-part verse alternates between a more reserved, off-beat section and a heavier counter part; 'Emergency' is generally more challenging than the previous two tracks. It plays with structure a little more, to its benefit; rather than rattling along at a blistering pace, beating the listener about the head with a series of hooks, its raw melodicism needs to be teased out with a little concentration. It's a great example of smart track placement – two straight down-the-line pop rock openers, and then a more expansive, demanding third track that nonetheless manages to keep the energy of the album intact. Of course, the chorus is nothing short of explosive.

Lyrically, it's amongst the most personal on the album, too. Unlike the saccharine tales of the redemptive and life-affirming love that is regularly the subject of pop songs, 'Emergency' deals with its darker side; a potentially restrictive, controlling and destructive force, which as Hayley notes, no one seems to want to talk about. "This song is about love, and not love in a good way. People have started to abuse love," Hayley told *Music Scene Media* when asked about the track. "I mean, it's becoming more and more common and you can see it with the divorce rates, and you can tell it by the way people

are treated. I see it all around and want to change it." Listening to the song, and hearing this comment, it's hard not to think of Hayley's personal experience with the break-up of her parents and the relationship between her mother and stepfather. She sings to a person who she has seen love beat down and harm all too often, and for one so young, it's disarmingly honest and confessional. Clearly, even at seventeen, Hayley was not afraid to pour her heart out on record for the benefit of her music.

Track four, 'Brighter', takes its foot off the gas a little, and at first listen seems somewhat tame in comparison to the previous three tracks. Despite being the fast end of mid-tempo, it seems to dawdle a little, the main riff innocuous, the verse slightly droning. But, once again, it is the chorus of 'Brighter' that saves it from being mere filler material. In fact, it boasts one of the most affecting choruses of the whole album, impassioned and heartfelt, but also with a real sense of melancholy. It's a sense that perfectly fits the lyrical content – the reluctance of moving on from a relationship that was meaningful and fulfilling, but has now run its course. Once again, Hayley's voice is magnificent: rich, robust, and full of sincere emotion.

'Here We Go Again' is the first track to really play around with the emotional rock formula that the album shows such a strong grasp of up to this point, and at track five, it feels like it needs it. For the first time Paramore offer a little in the way of groove, the syncopated drum beat working well with a slightly off-balance, casual guitar line. But it is also the first track to fall flat. Hayley's voice lacks the clarity and richness it has at other moments of *All We Know Is Falling*, and no melodies really jump out on first or subsequent listens. The dreary chorus feels emotionless, the instrumental guitar break like an uninspired run through. Fortunately, next track 'Never Let This Go' manages to get the album back on track, returning to safe ground with a reserved, elegantly plain verse and full-bodied rock chorus. The galloping drums of the chorus lend it an urgency as Hayley sings again of a failed relationship and the heartache that trying to cling onto it brings. It's not exactly a standout track, but it's a solid demonstration of what Paramore do.

With enthusiasm somewhat waning, it's a good job that the album really picks up pace towards its close. 'Whoa' is probably the finest song on the record, a shamelessly polished blend of everything that the rest of the album has showed them to be so good at: a tightly packed verse exploding into a mercilessly catchy chorus, anchored at the bottom by Zac Farro's machine-gun fire drumming and embellished at the top by Hayley's effortlessly athletic vocals. What's so good is the way it creeps up on the listener – Josh's opening guitar line almost sounds hesitant, pitched somewhere between downcast and hopeful, as Hayley sings of hoping for change and getting none. But the verse picks up momentum as Jason and Josh begin filling out the guitar sound, and we get a moment of silence to catch our breath before the most flirtatiously poppy moment of the record leaps out. It was definitely written with live shows in mind – you could just imagine a horde of rabid fans screaming "Whoa! Whoa-oh-oh!" at the top of their lungs at Hayley's behest – but it works brilliantly on record too, as riotous and uplifting a power-pop chorus as anything by New Found Glory or Blink-182.

Track eight is the first song Paramore ever wrote, 'Conspiracy'. It could so easily have been included because of sentimental attachment or as a nod to old fans. But amazingly, 'Conspiracy' is one of the more rewardingly slow-burning tracks on the album. Beginning with some crystalline guitar interplay before launching into keen and anxious power chord work, it has a singularly haunting quality. On first listen the immediacy of the rest of the album drowns it out, but on successive plays it comes into its own, the frantic drumming brilliantly accenting the themes of paranoia and persecution that the lyrics deal with. Immediately following this, and far more tender and affectionate, is 'Franklin', the band's love letter to their hometown. Some charming vocal interplay between Josh and Hayley on the chorus gives the song a sense of longing, and it is one of the more doleful tracks on the album, lacking the tension that gives some of the earlier tracks their urgency and power. It's a worthwhile addition to the album nonetheless, if only for the genuine pining you can hear in Hayley's voice as she sings of the difficulties of letting go of your hometown, and therefore, your childhood. It was inspired by the experience of moving to Orlando to record the album, and feeling that no one in Franklin had even noticed that they'd gone – "people in that town sort of didn't even know where the band was," Hayley said. "We were recording in Orlando and not many people, including some friends, knew where we were."

The album closer is 'My Heart', which sticks in the heads of most Paramore fans as the only song that has ever broached 'screamo' territory (an early version of 'Emergency' known as the 'Crab Mix' also featured Josh screaming some of Hayley's lines, but this version was not included on the album). On the chorus Josh Farro shows a clear debt to the likes of Thursday and really gives his vocal chords a thrashing, underpinning Hayley's almost cute vocals with an anguished, tortured roar. Other than this strange addition, 'My Heart' is a fairly straight down the line power-pop affair – wistful guitar playing, sentimental lyrics, and more than a little MOR. But just as if to hammer home their undeniable instinct for a great melody, right at the end of the album, they've squeezed in this final irresistible chorus, one that even the most toughened hardcore fan wouldn't be able to sneer at.

And so ends Paramore's first official release, *All We Know Is Falling*. At just over 35 minutes, it squeezes in around nine huge choruses and a whole heap of other deadly hooks and refrains that linger in the head for days; a huge dose of direct, power-chord riffery; a dynamic rhythm section powered by Zac Farro's spirited and forceful rock drumming; and of course, endless examples of why Hayley Williams was set to become one of the most recognisable voices (and faces) in modern rock music.

Yet the absence of Jeremy still weighed heavily on the band's mind, even after the completion of the record. In one interview Hayley noted how the photo seen on the back of the CD sleeve is from their first shoot after finishing the album and also therefore their first without Jeremy. While taking promo shots, the photographer had noticed a red couch in the abandoned lot behind his studio. He took the photo and, for the band, the image resonated and so ended up being the cover. "The actual concept behind the cover is emptiness," Hayley revealed to the *Music Scene Media* website. "It is to symbolise Jeremy not being a part of the band anymore. If you look there is a shadow walking away from the couch. That shadow is supposed to represent Jeremy walking away from what is Paramore." But even though they had essentially dedicated the front cover, title and opening track to their erstwhile bass player, touring demands meant Paramore needed to replace him. They recruited John Hembree, a friend from the Franklin area, as the new full-time bass player.

With the album completed and the template well and truly set, Paramore were ready to take on the outside world. Lucio Rubino, who recorded much of the bass on *All We Know Is Falling*, highlights another way that the band were preparing for their assault on the mainstream, a way which is often obscured from the general public's view. "Mark was really driving them hard," he revealed, referring to their manager Mark Mercado. "Making them eat healthy and run in the mornings. There was no monkey business. But that was good, y'know? They needed to be prepared, disciplined for what they were about to go through. Mark's a really great manager and a really great guy. They had a support group of a lot of really good and wise people to lead them in the right direction." When asked about how important he

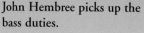
John Hembree picks up the bass duties.

believes a good management and support system for an artist, Lucio replied, "It's everything" – before qualifying himself. "Well, I wouldn't say it's everything. They have an amazing core of songwriting talent and ability, but everyone needs to be corralled a little bit by a strong support group, to put their energy into the right direction. And they had that. Supportive parents and great management." Lucio stresses that the band is in good hands with Mark Mercado: "He's not only very organised as a manager, but he's done the artistry thing too. So he knows the potential pitfalls that a band can have. He was in a band that had a moment when they were really popular, and he [also] saw it kind of crumble. So he knows what could happen to break it apart. I mean, it wasn't easy for them [Paramore], but they've done a good job of keeping it together."

But even the best manager in the world can't write a band's reviews. The media has a fairly contentious relationship with bands who deal in

Jason and Josh live in the early days.

emotionally fraught, pop-rock music, especially ones who are under twenty years old. Paramore were about to feel their first sting of the music press.

All We Know Is Falling was released on July 6, 2005 in the United States and April 26, 2006 in the UK. It would be a moderate success, selling some 50,000 copies in the United States and generating a fair amount of interest in the band (though since the release of its successor *Riot!*, the debut album has sold close to half a million copies and in 2008 it would appear at Number 8 in the UK albums chart, three years after its initial release). It would manage to reach Number 30 on the *Billboard* Heatseekers chart in September 2005, a chart intended to highlight the album sales of new and developing artists, though it failed to chart on the *Billboard* 200 (the main album sales listing in the USA). Much like the sales, critical response ranged from positive through to reserved, but also some fiercely critical. Hugely popular and influential UK rock and metal magazine *Kerrang!* was perhaps the most scathing of the mainstream publications. Giving the album two K's (out of a possible five), it said that Paramore deliver "perfectly formed emo-pop complete with a clean, clear production, bright, melodic guitars and songs that sound hook-laden as you listen to them but don't leave the slightest hint of a lasting impression... this is precisely the sound of style dancing on substance's grave." Rival British alternative mag *Rock Sound* was more positive, however, pointing out that Paramore are "only wee and need time to grow", and "worthwhile checking out… sooner rather than later," giving the album seven out of ten. But in truth, *All We Know Is Falling* arrived on the scene to little fanfare. Fueled By Ramen were advertising it alongside *Almost Here* by The Academy Is…, and Paramore were in danger of disappearing in the midst of a busy, even saturated new market. It is only since the release of *Riot!*, in fact, that many publications and websites have begun to take a retrospective and more look at *All We Know Is Falling*. In 2009 *Absolutepunk.net*, a popular site in the punk community for highlighting new artists, posted its first review of the album. The 'Final Verdict' was 78%, and one reviewer summed up his feelings by saying, "If you've never heard of it, listen to it now. You will surely be surprised, as I was, by just how good it is."

chapter 4

"THE TOUR THAT NEVER DIES"

For all Paramore's maturity and impressive professionalism on record, they could not help but occasionally let slip some small signs of their youth. The band had begun keeping a Live Journal (*Paramoreband.livejournal.com*): a blog, accessible to all and linked through their website, in which to keep fans informed of their movements and developments, both personal and professional. In May, Hayley posted an entry to explain her excitement at finishing the school year, telling the world how "my mom is out getting Starbucks and I hope she'll bring me back a soy chai or something." Of course, this is exactly what many sixteen-year-olds do on the day they finish school, or any other day – sit around waiting for someone to drop in. It's just that most sixteen-year-olds haven't just finished recording an album, and it's a strange juxtaposition, a rare occasion when you really get a sense of just how young the band were at this point.

And for ones so young, they found themselves having to deal with more harsh criticism from the bloodthirsty music press. The fact that the band boasts a highly talented and charismatic female vocalist was proving to be as much a source of dismissal as it was interest and, particularly at this stage of their career, the whole group found themselves having to defend against accusations that they were a pre-fabricated pop act. Zac probably offered the most convincing counter-argument, saying, "Think about it: [Why] would a label put us together if I was eleven years old and weighed, like, four hundred pounds? They wouldn't be like, 'Let's get that guy!'"

At the time of the release of *All We Know Is Falling*, a popular comparison for detractors was Avril Lavigne. The Canadian singer-songwriter had found huge commercial success with her debut album, *Let Go*, which has since been certified six-times platinum (denoting over six million sales). By 2005, the same year as the release of *All We Know Is Falling*, she had released her second album *Under My Skin*, which once again shifted huge numbers and produced numerous hit singles. But Lavigne has always been seen as a pop artist, regardless of her music being guitar driven, or the incorporation of punk fashion into her style (albeit watered down). An article in *Rolling Stone*, written after the release of *Let Go*, summed up the chagrin of many people, drawing attention to her "punk-rock-cred, or lack thereof," and that "Lavigne has been presented as a guitar-toting singer-songwriter. But it is unclear how much songwriting she does." For many, she was seen as the record industry's attempt to cash in on the increasing popularity of punk-pop. Bands like Blink-182 had made punk-pop big business, especially after their fourth album *Take Off Your Pants And Jacket* reached Number 1 in the *Billboard* charts in 2001, selling 350,000 copies in the first week of its release. But Blink-182 have retained a crude streak which makes them unpalatable for many people. Avril Lavigne represents a more inoffensive, acceptable alternative. Other female acts had followed suit, with a similar blend of guitar-based pop: the likes of Ashlee Simpson and Hilary Duff. For Paramore to play music somewhere in the arena of punk-pop, and have a female vocalist, comparisons were bound to be made, regardless of how different their music actually is. But the intent of those comparisons was usually to erroneously imply that Paramore were not credible as a rock band, artificially put together by some Machiavellian music mogul.

Initially, such comparisons understandably frustrated the band. In one interview the band reported that hostile crowd members would sometimes shout out requests for Lavigne songs – on one occasion Hayley even turned the tables by playing along, dropping lines from Lavigne's hit 'Sk8er Boi' into 'Here We Go Again'. Even before the release of *All We Know Is Falling*, Josh was posting on the band's LiveJournal in defence of Hayley's (patently vastly superior) vocal talents, a position which surely few would argue with. A few days later, Hayley would respond with a slightly more diplomatic and tentative approach to the topic. She stated that if she could be any pop star she would choose Avril, and that such comparisons were inevitable. She also stated that she is not out to be the next Avril and ends by hoping people will just see the band as a hard-working and authentic band. Paramore was about the get the opportunity to prove this, once and for all. They had a brand new album to promote.

To coincide with the release of *All We Know Is Falling*, Paramore chose

'Pressure' as their first single. John Janick already had a director in mind for the music video: Shane C. Drake had been at the helm of a handful of videos for bands in 2004, including screamo merchants Hawthorne Heights' 'Ohio Is For Lovers', and cult alt-rock band mewithoutYou's 'January 1979'. But he had also directed a promo for a little known Fueled By Ramen band called Fall Out Boy, a couple of years before their major label debut *From Under The Cork Tree* would take them to double platinum, Grammy-nominated superstardom. The song was 'Saturday', from their 2003 *Take This To Your Grave* album. Drake's video, which features bassist Pete Wentz executing members of the public and marking their bodies with playing cards, garnered the band some attention through airplay on music channels like FUSE and the MTVu college station. John Janick was obviously pleased with the results and keen to see what Drake could do with Paramore.

The band were all squashed in their van when word came through that they needed to come up with a concept for the video for 'Pressure'. It's a pretty simple premise: the band rocking out in what looks like a pump room (water/steam/pressure gauges), cut with a few examples of good-looking youths engaged in stressful situations. As the final chorus kicks in, one of the brow-beaten teens sets off the sprinklers, soaking the band and providing plenty of opportunity for cool slow-mo shots. But it's slick and well shot, and watching the band give it their all for their first video reveals no hint of nerves or awkwardness. They all look completely at ease in front of the camera lens, whether it's Zac theatrically smashing his cymbals, John Hembree rolling over Josh's back, or Hayley looking straight at the camera and giving a sly little half smile. Although the single failed to chart on the US *Billboard* Hot 100, airplay of the video on channels like Fuse TV did earn the band some much needed exposure.

Paramore had managed to get out on the road for a few shows whilst waiting for the release of the album. First they toured with Copeland (whom they'd played that first ever gig as openers for), and their fellow Floridians and labelmates Anberlin. Hayley would later offer a little dedication to those that witnessed Paramore on their first real tour, thanking them on the LiveJournal for giving the band a chance. They also made it out to the Cornerstone Festival in Illinois, a Christian music festival that showcases everything from hardcore to hip-hop to country and back again. But they were yet to begin touring in earnest, yet to experience a prolonged stretch in cramped conditions constantly promoting their record. Due to the timing of the release of *All We Know Is Falling*, they were then offered the best possible chance to make a name for themselves: a slot on the gruelling, chaotic, legendary Warped Tour.

One of many Warped Tour shows.

These days The Warped Tour (or the Vans Warped Tour, named after its skateboarding merchandise sponsor) stretches over three months and around 46 stop-offs, snaking around the USA from California to the south and then up through Indiana and Ohio to Canada; from there, down the East Coast (with a few diversions) to Florida, inland to Kansas, Idaho and Utah, back up for a couple of dates in Western Canada, and then back down through Washington to California. There are really no other festivals like it, none quite so demanding on its artists or so committed to covering every corner of the US. It has around ten stages that host roughly fifty bands per day, from 11a.m. to 9p.m. at night. It is more than a festival. It is something like a nomadic mecca, a punk pilgrimage that comes to you.

But it was not always so. It was dreamt up by just one man in the early 1990s: Kevin Lyman, a skateboarding enthusiast and LA club promoter who had worked on a handful of events combining extreme sports demonstrations and live music. For three years he worked as the stage manager for Lollapalooza, the alt-rock festival founded by Jane's Addiction's eccentric frontman, Perry Farrell. But in 1994 he decided to go his own way, taking the name 'Warped' from a short-lived extreme sports and culture magazine. Combining his love of southern Californian punk and summer weather, he rounded up the likes of female fronted ska outfit No Doubt (who would later reappear in Paramore's history) and Long Beach ska-punk-reggae fusioneers Sublime for a tour across the states. It was financially very stressful, and Lyman was seriously considering abandoning the project for the following year, but he gave it one more try. For the second year, No Doubt and Sublime once again appeared as headliners, but the bill extended beyond sun-kissed, laid-back ska-punk. It found room, amongst others, for Sacramento alternative metallers Deftones, hardcore punk bruisers Sick Of It All, post-hardcore trendsetters Quicksand and all-female grunge act L7. But despite the increased size of the festival, the no-nonsense punk ethic was still very much in evidence – bands like Sublime and Orange 9mm, L7 and No Use For A Name shared tour buses to cut costs.

In 1996, Lyman was approached to tour manage a skate tour for Vans, and proposed combining extreme sports demonstrations with live punk and rock music, which had long been the soundtrack to those scenes anyway. And so, in 1996, the Vans Warped Tour was born. The capital and impetus of the Vans label allowed Lyman to get heavyweight punk acts like NOFX and

Pennywise on the bill. From there on in, the Vans Warped Tour grew exponentially. By 1998 it was taking punk godfathers Bad Religion and upstarts The Get Up Kids overseas on international dates, and had earned itself a reputation as the "tour that never dies" for its ceaseless trekking all over the States. It would help to launch the careers of countless bands, so much so that unsigned acts had begun attempting to sneak in, helping out as crew or catering and then jumping on stage. Sometimes bands even just rolled up in the parking lot with a generator.

But as the Vans Warped Tour moved into the new Millennium, it attracted a number of controversies and criticisms in hand with its success. One of these was cynicism about its sheer size, which to many seemed in opposition to the DIY punk ethic. Others accused the Warped Tour of stifling the summer tour circuit, as acts felt the pinch of dwindling ticket sales when competing with the tour; others berated what they saw as old-fashioned commercialism due to the number of corporate sponsors. But Lyman strongly defends the choice of allowing corporate sponsors in on the Warped Tour, saying that a lot of the money they provide goes towards helping bands get the support they need to complete a massive stint like Warped. One particularly memorable case is of the original tour sponsors, Vans, who weren't even allowed to have a banner on stage until four years into their sponsorship. And when they finally were, it was a band (rumoured to be MxPx) not Lyman, that made that call – because Vans head of marketing Steve Van Doren had built a personal relationship, providing the band members with clean socks.

But perhaps the most frequent criticism of the Warped Tour has been levelled at the changing line-ups. In an interview with *The Wire*, Joe Queer, singer of veteran 1980s punk act the Queers, famously slighted the tour's move away from more traditional punk acts to the kaleidoscopic variations on the genre that it now hosted. "You play music because there's something inside of you that says you have to play music," he said, citing Green Day as a band who have achieved commercial success and stayed true to themselves. "The Warped Tour changed it. I just don't like that shit. All the guys in the bands remind me of the jocks I hated in high school." But Lyman defended his choice of the changing line-ups, stating that the Warped Tour was never intended as solely a punk affair: "When you think about who was on the first year," he explained on the *Punknew.org* website, "L7, No Doubt, Sublime,

Quicksand, CIV, Orange 9mm, No Use For A Name – it was very reflective of what was going on at that time, but those bands can't be placed into one category. Musically, it was pretty diverse back then. In 1996, when NOFX and Pennywise came out with me, it became recognised because of these larger bands as a punk tour." It was a deliberate decision to move with the times and represent what is current in music alongside veteran punk acts, as he explained: "The Warped Tour has never been for that ten percent that considered itself completely gutter punk." These were the kind of concerns and debates flying around when Paramore joined the tour in 2005.

That year's tour started on July 20. Paramore were alongside what was essentially a roster of popular American guitar-based music at the time. Two of the big hits of the tour that year would go on to represent, at least in the media's eyes, the new face of 'emo'. On the one hand, there was Fall Out Boy – awkward, overly-sensitive and overly-brainy, with a surprisingly broad array of influences and a tendency toward elaborate, tongue-in-cheek lyrical conceits. They were touring in release of their major label debut, *From Under The Cork Tree*, which was speeding them from a relatively popular alternative act to world-beaters. On the other hand, there was My Chemical Romance, who performed on stage in bulletproof vests, took a more direct influence from hardcore punk and metal, and whose lyrics dealt brazenly with themes like depression and death. The previous year they had released their breakthrough album *Three Cheers For Sweet Revenge*, and as they took off that band would become in many people's eyes the (unwilling) poster boys of 'emo'. They would also come to represent what some hysterical sections of the media saw as an anti-social, morose, sour and even suicidal generation in love with self-pity. In 2006 *The Daily Mail* would spark controversy by warning parents against the "emo cult" that celebrates self-harm, and then in 2008, repeatedly mentioned My Chemical Romance in an article blaming the suicide of a thirteen-year-old girl on her love of emo music. Of course, this was all a long way off in 2005, but both bands were there alongside Paramore on the Warped Tour, their careers both about to go stellar: Fall Out Boy, the tragic jesters; My Chemical Romance, the black knights.

But there was much else on offer that year, of course. A variety of more established, straight-down-the-line punk acts were alongside the new generation of tabloid-bait: the likes of The Offspring, MxPx and Strung Out. There was also a slew of bands that had taken the early 1990s emo

template and merged it with heavy metal riffery – bands like Thrice, Senses Fail and Funeral For A Friend.

Paramore were booked to play on the ShiraGirl stage, a platform devoted to female-fronted bands. It had been established the previous year, when ShiraGirl – a punk-come-hip-hip-electro act – decided to rectify the distinct lack of female involvement in the festival by rocking up unannounced and performing from the back of their RV. Kevin Lyman walked past mid-set, but instead of kicking them out, invited them onto the tour for a few more dates. By the time the tour was over, ShiraGirl had presented an official proposal to host their own stage, and provide a platform for all-female or female-fronted bands to perform. It was Paramore's first big tour and undoubtedly somewhat overwhelming for them, though in retrospect, they remember being a little disappointed seeing the size of the festival and then seeing the ShiraGirl stage. "I think we were kind of bummed the first day when we saw how big the other stages were and how much louder the PAs were," Hayley revealed to *Alternative Press*. They were first on a bill of bands that have since largely struggled to launch themselves into the mainstream public consciousness, though the likes of Gina Young and Midway are still gigging. Despite the inauspicious start, once the tour got underway, Paramore became swept up in the excitement of it. They even started to see people singing the words to the songs back to them. Even at these early shows, Paramore were attracting fans that would stick with them throughout their career. At the Warped Tour date in Minnesota, one Ashley Brown would be amongst the crowd of "roughly fifteen" people for Paramore's set. "The people that were there for them knew who they were," she recalled for this book. "Like ten people who knew who they were and five people who didn't. They were itty-bitty, they were like fifteen and fourteen years old, so they were super young. Hayley sounded really good though, they sounded good, even though it was just a little platform stage. They did some signings by the booth after and we talked for a little bit." Ashley, who works as a web designer for ad agencies, instantly fell in love with the band and in late August of the same year she founded the excellent web community *paramorefans.com*. She still runs it today – except now it has around 8,000 members. She has seen the band over thirty times.

On the Warped Tour, the standard length of a set is thirty minutes, and Paramore were determined to give the best possible show they could. As the tour went on, they began to feel more confident about their thirty minutes, being comfortable with the performance they could deliver in such a small window of time. But they had some other tactics for winning over potential fans, and they weren't work shy. Every morning before their show, they would be out flyering and trying to convince kids to wander over to the ShiraGirl stage to catch their set. One patron remembers that in that year, the festival ground was littered with Paramore flyers. Confrontational kids would knock the flyers out of their hands or even spit on them, but Paramore weren't perturbed. They were just determined to draw a crowd for their set. Seeing all of the bands that they personally loved on other stages, drawing crowds of one or two thousand must have been a strange feeling. "That's just something that's incredible to us," Hayley reveals. But they never doubted that they would reach a similar level of success or even beyond: "We'll get there. We don't put pressure on ourselves, and just have a great time." Their tactics were working, too, because at every show their crowds were getting bigger and bigger – they remember New Jersey as the best stop-off on the tour, with somewhere close to 400 spectators at the ShiraGirl Stage for their slot. One reviewer for *The Trades*, a US-based entertainment website, had the foresight to seek out Paramore at the Pompano Beach, Florida leg of the tour. Tony Pascarella writes of how people began drifting toward the stage once they began their set: "Before you knew it, there were probably over a hundred people crowded around the stage, some singing along, some trying to learn the lyrics as they heard the songs... I highly recommend Paramore, if you haven't found that out yet: they've got a ton of talent and they're going places." In the midst of all this activity, Paramore still took a couple of days off to play a free in-store show at an independent record store in Franklin. Working relentlessly has never been something that the band are afraid of.

A couple of weeks before the tour had started, Hayley posted a message on Paramore's LiveJournal revealing that new bassist John Hembree would be missing a couple of dates to attend a friend's wedding. Needing a fill in, they had asked their old band mate Jeremy if he would come and rehearse with them and fill in for John in his absence. Jeremy jumped at the chance. He had been working for Dominoes pizza and selling knives door-to-door, while he watched his former band slowly but steadily increase in popularity. But the band had been missing him too. It is unclear as to the exact time-frame of when Jeremy was offered a return to the official line-up but needless to say when he was asked to join once again, he readily accepted. He recalls receiving the news: "I remember I was at a car shop and I was trying to act like it wasn't a big deal. I was like, 'Yeah, let me think about it…'" Needless to say, as soon as he put the phone down he let his relief show! Despite the rough time he had had back in Franklin, he claims that he doesn't regret having left the band in the first place. "It was a big mistake," he says, "but I wouldn't take it back because I learnt how much I love these guys and how much it all means to me. Even when I was home, I learnt some lessons that are pretty valuable in my life. So I think it all happened for a reason."

With the band back to its original line-up, they continued touring after the completion of the Warped Tour. First they hit the road with Bedlight For Blue Eyes and My American Heart. Paramore would frequently mention My American Heart as one of their favourite bands to tour with after this initial meeting. In September they played The Icon venue in Buffalo, and Zac was so pleased with the show he took to LiveJournal to enthuse about it as one of the best shows they had ever played. At the completion of this tour, they immediately set out again, this time with Seattle alternative rockers Acceptance in support of their 2005 release *Phantoms* (which would turn out to be their last). In support with Paramore was The Receiving End Of Sirens, who had also appeared on the 2005 Warped Tour and introduced Hayley to some of the finer points of success: she declared on LiveJournal that Acceptance's RV was like a home-from-home and wondered, genuinely, if Paramore would ever be successful enough to own one.

With sales of both *All We Know Is Falling* and their live momentum picking up, in November of 2005 Paramore were booked on a tour with Simple Plan. The Quebec pop-punkers had formed in 1999, but their 2004 sophomore effort, *Still Not Getting Any…*, had far outstripped their debut in terms of sales and exposure. It had been produced by the irrepressible Bob Rock, who had been the man at the controls for most of Metallica's 1990s revival, and they would be playing throughout October and November in support. The tour also featured Straylight Run, an indie-rock outfit hailing from Long Island and featuring former members of Taking Back Sunday, and Plain White T's (who would go on to enjoy massive success with their single 'Hey There Delilah' some three years later). The tour stretched over 13 dates, beginning in San Deigo and ending in Los Angeles, visiting a variety of concert venues up to 8,000 in capacity. It would be the largest production Paramore had been involved with to date, but they were just happy that for the first time they were allowed to eat the venue's catering. The day before they played New York, they also received word that their video for 'Pressure' had reached Number 1 on Fuse TV's 'Oven Fresh', a chart which users vote for through Fuse's website. The cult of Paramore had begun.

Their next booking was with Welsh emo-metallers Funeral For A Friend in December, after a brief stop-off at home for Thanksgiving. But much to everyone's disappointment – Josh had expressed his love of the band – the tour was cancelled, as drummer Ryan Richards contracted a stomach infection and was unable to travel. Still, Paramore were determined to use their first real stint of time off constructively, and were already looking toward a new album. Josh had started penning a few new song ideas, so they used the time to "recharge" and have a go at pulling some new material together.

While Paramore were on this break, Fueled By Ramen released a new demo they had recorded in their down-time on a compilation CD. Entitled 'This Circle' (and not 'Circle' as Hayley was quick to point out), it's quite a development of the sound from *All We Know Is Falling*: opening with a clipped and clean riff, Zac's off-beat drumming kicks in alongside some shimmering, surf guitar. It's a refreshingly breezy sound that they never really strived for on their debut. The chorus introduces a little more strife and discordance, with Hayley's distinctive and ever captivating wails slicing through the mix. The whole song is a little off-balance – the transitions from verse to bridge to chorus, each with their own distinctive flavour, perhaps feel a little clunky – but it is a great example of the band playing around with their sound, looking for where to go next. It almost seems to have half a foot in the post-rock world, drawing influence from sonically experimental rock bands like Seattle's Minus The Bear. It is the sound of a band chomping at the bit to move their music forward.

But moving forward sometimes requires change, as Paramore already knew too well. After Jeremy returned to the fold, they had probably hoped that their line-up change dramas were done for good, but they had no such luck. On December 16, 2005, as the band was coming to the end of their first year as a professional group, they posted a statement on their LiveJournal announcing that Jason Bynum would be leaving the band.

He had joined Paramore very soon after its inception and spent two years as a full time member, yet he felt it was time to leave. Paramore were keen to emphasise that the split had been amicable: "Just so everyone knows, up front, there is no bad blood between us. Jason left on really good terms and he will be dearly missed." No reason or explanation was offered as to why Bynum had taken the decision to leave the band, with things seemingly moving so quickly in the right direction. But Paramore already knew only too well that in the face of such challenges, the best course of action was to push on regardless.

chapter 5

ACROSS THE POND

Paramore soon announced that a new member had been found, and would be introducing himself through the LiveJournal. That new member was William "Hunter" Lamb, who announced his arrival to the increasingly fanatical Paramore fanbase with the cheerful words, "Hey guys, this is Hunter. I'm really happy to be a part of the band now!" Hunter, a native of Franklin, Tennessee, and an old friend of the band, had previously been playing with local band Our Heart's Hero who had earned a modest following with their straightforward, epic pop-rock and strong Christian message. Hunter had played in the band with his twin brother Hayden on drums. Hayden would go on to play with Nashville Christian hard rock act Red, but left in 2007 after their van crashed, rendering him unable to complete the tour.

Next up, Paramore filmed the promo for what would be their second single from *All We Know Is Falling*, the explosive 'Emergency'. Shane Drake was once again at the top of their list of directors: "We're hoping if we do a new video, he'd be interested in doing it with us, because he's incredible," said Hayley. Despite enjoying the experience of filming the 'Pressure' promo, they were sure their second would be an improvement. "We love the video and how it turned out, but we're just going to make our next one a whole lot better," Josh had said after completing the 'Pressure' video. And sure enough, the 'Emergency' video is a big leap forward from 'Pressure', which was, as Hunter brilliantly puts it, "this happy 'I spilled the milkshake' video." It avoids the obvious clichés of an angsty teen promo and strives for something a little darker and more compelling. It opens with the band, dressed in torn and dirty evening-wear and each sporting a carnation, in an abandoned and derelict house. They are all covered in cuts and bruises, and an early shot sees Josh washing his face of rusty blood. As a man comes in and tosses Hayley

Bynum's replacement Hunter Lamb.

some flowers, they are led outside: he is revealed to be the video's director, and after their mocked-up injuries are touched up for the cameras, they get the signal to start performing. This they do with aplomb, Hayley having perfected her eyes closed, lost-in-the-music shimmy and Josh and Hunter throwing their guitars about as if they were toys. Fan forums were awash with theories as to what the video actually meant, the most popular interpretation seeming to be something about the wounds the band bear – representing emotional baggage – and the way the group is forced to parade these scars around for the benefit of their careers. As Hayley says, "It's very much about imagery and it's abstract. It's not really something you can watch and just get. I think it will leave people guessing." It seems just as likely, perhaps, that it all just looked really cool. But either way, the video would help 'Emergency' far outstrip 'Pressure' in terms of success, and win the band more exposure.

The single was released on October 2005 and featured 'Oh Star' as the B-side. In September of that year, 'Oh Star' had been released as an exclusive with the Japanese version of *All We Know Is Falling*, but here it was made available to US fans for the first time. In contrast to 'This Circle', it's a straightforward, wistful ballad, with big melodic hooks and a typically anthemic chorus. In the bridge, Hayley really demonstrates the range and strength of her voice, leaping around the octaves with an enviable ease while the music gives her the space to do so. But other than that, it feels like a track that there wasn't really any space for on *All We Know Is Falling*, just a little too innocuous, a little too much like filler material. Nonetheless, 'Emergency' and its accompanying music video did well for the band. While it failed to chart on the *Billboard* 100, it received a lot of play on alternative music channels like FUSE in the US and *Kerrang!* TV and MTV2 in the UK.

With the year coming to a close, more and more people were becoming aware of a surprisingly young melodic rock band peddling an impressive arsenal of tunes, captained by the tiny fire-haired girl with a voice that could level a house. There was no doubt that Paramore's star was in the ascendancy but they were determined to keep their noses to the grindstone and tour relentlessly with rest of the punk rock dogs of war.

The relentless promotion of *All We Know Is Falling* showed no sign of slowing in the New Year. In January, after two months relaxing, they set out on the first of many tours that year, ready to get back on the road – their absence only seemed to have heightened demand for them to play. This time

they were heading out with DC punkers Amber Pacific, now defunct Tooth & Nail outfit Terminal, and Seattle pop-rockers The Lashes. The jaunt was dubbed the 'Winter Go West Tour', and stretched from January 19 to February 4. After this they immediately segued into a tour with Californian four-piece Halifax. But just a few dates into the tour, Paramore were struck by a recurring problem that would intermittently harass the band throughout their career. A LiveJournal post dated February 18 revealed that on top of delays caused by icy roads, Hayley had woken up unable to speak. The strains of rigorous touring, cold weather and late shows had taken their toll on her vocal cords, and the only effective treatment was for Hayley to rest her voice. They assured fans that they would make the show up to them, and after a couple of days, the band were back in action.

Next up was a slot on the 'Take Action! Tour'. Established in 1999, it is a spring tour (beginning in March) that aims to raise awareness regarding a variety of issues affecting young people through music. The band were extremely enthusiastic about playing the tour, especially in light of its charitable function, but Hayley's voice would foil them again, and this time a couple of days' rest was not quite enough to get her back on her feet again. She would require several weeks off and a course of antibiotics, resulting in the cancellation of most of the 'Take Action! Tour' (they had only managed to play the first date in Washington D.C. on February 21). The band then released the third and final single from their debut: 'All We Know'. The video was directed by Dan Dobi and is a montage of live and backstage footage filmed on their tour.

After a few weeks' rest, the band were ready to continue on with their unremitting trekking around the US in promotion of *All We Know Is Falling*. The next booking was in support of Bayside, a New York punk rock outfit that had attracted something of a cult following after the release of their debut album, *Sirens And Condolences*. At the end of 2005 Bayside had been forced to contend with tragedy as their van hit some ice on the road, the subsequent crash killing drummer John 'Beatz' Holohans. But in the great tradition of hard-working punk bands, the best consolation was to hit the road again, and Paramore joined them as openers on a stretch that lasted from April 3 to 9.

To close out that month, Paramore had a big treat in store: their first ever trip to the UK for the 'Give It A Name Festival', which would be taking place over two days at Earl's Court in London, and the MEN Arena, Manchester. The first 'Give It A Name' had only taken place the year before, headlined by Welsh screamo merchants Funeral For A Friend and also featuring Finch, Alexisonfire and one of Hayley's favourite bands, mewithoutYou. But it had been so successful that for the second year it had been spread over two different dates in two cities, and was boosted with a main and second stage. Gracing the main stage were Paramore's Warped co-tourers, My Chemical Romance and Welsh power-rock six-piece Lostprophets, but the bill also featured a host of other contemporary rock acts: Blink-182 member Tom Delonge's space-rock vehicle Angels And Airwaves, tumultuous alternative rockers Taking Back Sunday, Fueled By Ramen darlings Panic! At The Disco and LA punk stalwarts Goldfinger were but a few. The second stage was headlined by Canadian firebrands Billy Talent and British indie-rockers Hundred Reasons, although rock-hip-hop fusioneers and fellow Fueled By Ramen act Gym Class Heroes would also make an appearance. In support of the main dates in Manchester and London, Paramore went off on the 'Give It A Name Introduces… Tour', to smaller venues in Cardiff, Birmingham, Glasgow, Newcastle and Liverpool. Hayley felt that the UK was a real defining moment for the band, posting on the band's LiveJournal that she felt the band had evolved dramatically and were already a new and improved version. Amongst the joys of the UK that particularly stayed with her included eating Shepherd's pie in a Wetherspoons pub, hearing a genuine Scottish accent and getting their van broken into in Wales. But the tour was a massive success for the band, with a rabid response from fans on their first real overseas trip. At the London date, a few members of the band made an appearance at their merchandise stall after their set. The word spread like wildfire amongst Paramore zealots and before long they had incited a mini state of emergency, with fans excitedly mobbing them. Their only means of escape was to be escorted out by members of the security staff. They had had their first real taste of so-called Paramania. The actual performance was a huge success too, despite the band being slightly overwhelmed by the size of the gig. "It was the first huge crowd we'd ever played in front of so we were really nervous," said Josh to *Kerrang!*. But the show went well, and the sheer size of the audience was a source of pride for the band. The band returned to the US triumphant. They had conquered their first dominion.

One more tour awaited Paramore upon returning to their homeland, before they would have to confront the next looming, Warped Tour-shaped shadow on the horizon. In the meantime, they made an appearance at the Bamboozle tour in New Jersey, where they were once again mobbed at their merchandise stand (a scenario that was becoming increasingly familiar). As a barometer of their rapidly increasing reputation, and no doubt a result of their tireless touring since the release of *All We Know Is Falling*, Hayley estimates there were somewhere close to 3,000 people in the crowd for Paramore's set. They had come a long way in less than a year, when they were struggling to get three hundred people to watch them at the previous Warped Tour. Next they played a hefty string of dates on tour with The Rocket Summer, the moniker of multi-instrumentalist and vocalist Bryce Avary, at a variety of mid-sized venues.

The next step was for Paramore to set out on the Warped Tour. This time around they would be mainly playing on the Volcom and Hurley stages: not yet the main stage, but better located and more likely to draw a crowd all the same. Joining them this time were many of the bands that had appeared the previous year, as well as a few newcomers: Fueled By Ramen bands like The Academy Is… and Gym Class Heroes, long-standing punk acts like Anti-Flag and NOFX, and heavier acts like Every Time I Die and Alexisonfire.

Realising that they could do with something else to promote, they put together *The Summer Tic EP*, a four-track CD featuring, in order, 'Emergency (The Crab Mix)', 'Oh Star', 'Stuck On You' and 'This Circle'. The Crab Mix of 'Emergency' is much the same as the version on the album. The main difference is that Josh screams under Hayley's singing during sections of the verse. The band revealed that they had named the song in honour of the producer of that mix, Pete Thornton, who shuffled like a crab whilst playing ping pong. 'Stuck On You' is a cover of 1990s alt-rockers Failure, who Josh has cited as a major influence on him during his formative years. It's a moody, mid-tempo track, that goes in some strange melodic directions, slowly unfolding as you allow it to sink in. A line from the song also lends the EP its title.

As the tour rumbled into motion, Paramore were seeing their success reflected more and more in the response of their audiences. Even as early as their tour with Simple Plan in 2005, they had felt the way crowds reacted to them was changing; from indifference to enthusiasm to out-and-out fervour. To many, Paramore were no longer a teenage band trying to make their mark. They were card-carrying rock stars. They had also added a little theatre to their stage show, wearing the red carnations on their clothes that were to appear in the 'Emergency' video. As the tour stopped off in Nashville, on June 21, Warped founder Kevin Lyman promoted the band to the main stage for their first hometown performance in months. One reviewer for *drivenfaroff.com* noted that "they have never put on a bad show in Nashville, and they continued their streak… Front-woman Hayley Williams may be small, but she knows how to command a crowd better than a lot of bands headlining this tour for multiple years." It was the band's first taste of real Warped Tour esteem and Hayley excitedly posted an entry that night on the band's LiveJournal as a tribute to the gig. The band also got the chance to play on the main stage at the Orlando stop-off, and though it wasn't quite the same reaction as the Nashville date, they enjoyed it all the same.

There was plenty of opportunity for fun and frolics, too. Since first meeting My American Heart on the 2005 Warped tour, they and Paramore had become close friends, and would often name each other as a favourite band to tour with. At the San Francisco date, Paramore did a signing at the Super Soaker tent, and were paid with a veritable arsenal of water guns. Boys will be boys, as they say, and the male members of the band decided that they were going to test out their new weaponry live and in the field (so to speak). They headed down to the Ernie Ball stage while My American Heart were playing their set and unleashed litres of fury at their pals. But all actions have consequences, and a few days later at the Ventura, California leg of the tour, retribution came whilst Paramore were doing a signing in the *Alternative Press* tent. Armed with water balloons, My American Heart ambushed them and got their revenge. You can watch the (very funny) video on YouTube – a particular highlight is drummer Steven Oira giving the warning, "Paramore – can you feel the pressure?"

Yet for all the high spirited pranks and gathering commercial momentum, the Warped Tour would also play host to some darker moments for Paramore…

Paramore with Hunter celebrating Jeremy's birthday.

chapter 6

"THE FIRST PARAMORE"

Things were coming along very nicely on the Warped Tour, with crowd sizes getting steadily bigger, but it was not without its drama. One standout moment came whilst travelling to a show in the North, when in the small hours of the morning the band's van hit a deer so hard it "pooped" all down the side of their trailer. You imagine they weren't too popular pulling up in the midday heat the following morning. At the Tampa date, Hunter got a little too involved and fell off the stage while jumping from a speaker. He somehow managed to land on his feet, but he couldn't quite carry it off with the conviction to make it look deliberate. He remembers it as one of the most embarrassing moments of the tour.

Another memorable event occurred at the Miami leg. Prior to their set, Paramore had been hanging out at the merchandise tent, signing autographs and taking pictures for what they reckoned was the longest line they had ever had. At this point the sun was beating down remorselessly, as it tends to do throughout the Warped Tour – "burning us alive", as Hayley put it. In fact, the line was so long that the band were drawing ever closer to their allotted slot, and had to cut the signings a little short. But as soon as they took to the stage, ominous dark clouds had gathered. The heavens opened and it rained with the kind of determination that can only be described as an act of God, bringing the entire festival – including Paramore's set – to a grinding halt. But the fans stayed anyway, battling nature's fury and chanting for Paramore to continue playing until the band were finally forced to leave. Hayley would later commemorate the event with a small tattoo behind her left ear – an old school-style design of a black cloud with a bolt of lightning striking from it, with the word 'WARPED!' inscribed in plain script above.

On this tour Hayley also experienced – not for the first time – animosity directed at her for being one of just a few females performing on a stage usually dominated by men. At a stop-off in Fresno, California, Hayley had a condom thrown at her by a member of the crowd. "A lot of embarrassing moments are just funny," she commented in an interview with *paramorefans.com*, hinting that this situation was not one of them. "Dude, and it like stuck to my gross sweaty chest. And seriously, it was pretty embarrassing. I'll be honest, I got a little upset at that moment." While Paramore could not deny that the simple novelty of having a female front-woman has gained them much exposure throughout their career, this was not the first time Hayley had experienced some resistance towards her because of her gender. Right from the word go it had been evident, with those people dismissing Paramore and Hayley as another Avril clone intended for the pop market. Hayley even claimed on *europunk.net* that the guys in the band were "edgy about the whole female thing" before they all became comfortable writing and playing together. But of course, Hayley is not the first woman to enter the predominantly male world of rock music – in fact, she belongs to a small but extremely influential lineage of female artists.

So if Avril Lavigne isn't the right parallel for Hayley, who is? And what kind of artists set the precedent for women to be taken seriously in the rock world? For many, Janis Joplin was the first female singer in rock to really make a mark. She started out as the singer of Big Brother and the Holding Company in the late 1960s, who had emerged from the Haight-Ashbury hippie community in San Francisco. Their bluesy, psychedelic rock was progressive and interesting, but it was Joplin's incredibly emotive, expressive wail that really turned heads. In 1968 their album *Cheap Thrills*, which features an incredible version of 'Summertime' and 'Piece of My Heart', hit Number 1. Shortly after Joplin split from the band and embarked on a solo career, which ended with her premature death in 1970. Around the same time, Jefferson Airplane were making headway with their own brand of psychedelic rock, and in 1966 they were joined by former model Grace Slick as lead singer. Her voice might not have had the raw power of Joplin's (with whom Slick remained friends up to her death), but she was beautiful, intelligent and a great songwriter. Rock 'n' Roll wasn't very old, but by the end of the 1960s, it could already boast two captivating and hugely influential daughters.

But from here, and for whatever reason, the appearance of truly iconic female artists in rock music has been irregular at best. In America in 1975,

Fleetwood Mac's classic self-titled album would launch the career of Stevie Nicks, and Patti Smith would release her debut *Horses* and earn herself the title of 'Godmother of punk'. On the other side of the Atlantic, towards the end of the decade and into the 1980s, Chrissie Hynde would lead The Pretenders to critical and commercial success. But of all these hugely different, highly important female artists, perhaps the best known, and most akin to Hayley, is Debbie Harry of Blondie. Born in Miami, Florida, but adopted at three months and moved to New Jersey, she would spend her youth in a variety of different employments. Like Hayley she was young when Blondie formed, though she was out of her teens. Blondie would come together in the creative and influential New York punk scene, centred around the CBGB's club. Patti Smith would also regularly play there, alongside The Ramones and Television. Much like Hayley, Harry formed a fruitful and enduring songwriting partnership with a man, named Chris Stein, and their debut album *Blondie* would be released in 1976. Mainstream success would not come until 1978, however, with the release of their third album *Parallel Lines*, which spawned the classic singles 'Hanging On The Telephone' and 'Heart Of Glass'.

With Blondie's commercial success also came a widespread fascination with Harry. Her distinctive looks – bleach blonde hair, sharp bone structure and piercing blue eyes – was coupled with a unique fashion sense, which was feminine and elegant yet effortlessly cool. And much like Paramore, Blondie would find that the band were often pushed aside by the media, who preferred to focus attention on their front-woman. In 1979, Blondie would produce and distribute buttons featuring the slogan 'Blondie is a group'. Paramore's first printed T-shirts would read, 'Paramore is a band'. As Josh explains, the increasing success of Paramore was only exacerbating the obsession with Hayley and the neglect of her band mates: "We knew that it would just get worse the more fans we gain. People are going to be more focused on Hayley. It happens with any lead man, but it's a little different because she's a girl. There are times when it just happens so much that we are like, 'Oh man, this is getting annoying.'" But Josh believes that the band's image of itself is more important than the way others look at it. "Deep down we know that we are a band and that's how we see ourselves," he said to *Absolutepunk.net*. "As long as people know that's how we feel and who we are." In 2008 Hayley would get to meet Debbie Harry at the Woodie's Award

Ceremony, and tell her predecessor how important her work with Blondie had been. She also added that she doubted Paramore would have been able to achieve what they had without Blondie's success. Despite fearing that Harry merely thought she was "kissing ass," Hayley remembers it as a "great moment" and one that she will never forget.

The late 1980s saw a lull in the presence of powerful women in rock music, largely because the main movement at the time was the testosterone-fuelled machismo nonsense of cock rock, which most women musicians obviously weren't pre-disposed to be involved with. The grunge movement which mercifully banished cock rock from the airwaves had L7, an all-female band whose third album *Bricks Are Heavy* was produced by Butch Vig (also responsible for Nirvana's *Nevermind*). The 1990s also gave us Courtney Love, of course; while her band Hole's second album *Live Through This* garnered many positive reviews and hefty album sales, selling over two million copies worldwide, Hole would eventually decline in popularity and ultimately split in 2002.

So at the time Paramore came to prominence, there was a gaping hole in the market for a genuinely captivating, credible, and talented female artist in the rock arena. Evanescence and singer Amy Lee had found success in 2003

with huge sales of their debut *Fallen*, but their gothic rock trappings were really hiding a very dull sound, and they failed to maintain their initial popularity. Similarly, Lacuna Coil had begun to receive some attention from magazines like *Kerrang!*, but probably more for the opportunity to put striking front-woman Christina Scabbia in the pages rather than their somewhat dated nu-metal sound. The closest thing to a real superstar in the recent arena had been Gwen Stefani, who had featured on the very first Warped Tour with her band No Doubt. In the early days No Doubt had been influenced by Two Tone acts like The Specials and Madness, and set about producing their own modern, American take on the genre. Their third album *Tragic Kingdom* had a difficult birth – it took over three years to make – but it would catapult them to global fame, mostly off the back of the Number 1 single 'Don't Speak'. After a couple more albums, Stefani continued to make interesting music but as a solo artist, and definitely no longer in the world of rock.

Alternative music was really crying out for Hayley Williams at the time of her arrival – though initially, it must be said, only a few people saw the potential of a superstar in the seventeen-year-old. In 2006, writer and Fuse TV VJ Steven Smith wrote that seeing Paramore play reminded him of No Doubt in the early days of their career. "Gwen Stefani and her band mates didn't know it yet," he writes, "but something big was happening. Paramore have the same feeling. Hayley Williams is a star on the mic, and her and her band mates are going to morph from super-talented musicians to all around bad asses before you know it." Despite his foresight, you get the impression that all comparisons are, for Hayley, a little misleading. On the Gwen Stefani associations, she said, "I'm really flattered to hear those things. I like Gwen Stefani as part of No Doubt. We'll see what happens, but we want to be the first Paramore." In fact, one of the most important aspects of Hayley's approach is not that she cleverly manipulates or uses her status as one of only a few females in a male dominated genre. It is the opposite – that she is, if not unaware, then at least dismissive of it. As Hayley stated in an interview with *Music Scene Media* in 2006: "We, as a band, are confident as to who we are and what we are doing, and people need to respect that. Many people tell me, 'You are the only girl that fronts a band that I like.' That proves something about Paramore that other bands aren't doing. I'm not doing this to start a movement; we are doing this because I love it and the dudes love it." The band were all aware that having a female lead singer was different and going to be pushed by everyone who wanted to sell the band. But the key thing for Paramore was knowing that they aren't a female-fronted rock band: they're a rock band whose singer happens to be female.

This distinction is very important in understanding both the band's, and Hayley's appeal. While Paramore were clearly getting frustrated with the inordinate amount of attention placed on Hayley, it is worth looking at why she has inspired so much attention. Firstly, she has always been outspoken that she has no intention of using her sex appeal as a tool to sell Paramore's music. She's beautiful, and there's no getting around that – but her charm and on-stage persona is more punk rock girl-next-door than femme fatale. As she said to *Kerrang!* in 2006, "I dress quite conservatively. There's no midriff showing, or cleavage." She adds that the team around her put no pressure on her to sex up her image for the sake of sales. The only pressure she feels, if any, is from herself – particularly when compared to Gwen Stefani, who is known almost as much for her washboard stomach as she is for her music. But at the end of the day, Hayley is wise enough to know that regardless of what she sees around her, she has to go her own way: "We're not going to get anywhere if we're not true to who we are."

Sex appeal and punk rock are not necessarily at opposite ends of the spectrum. Debbie Harry combined the two with ease, for example, but only because it was an expression of her personality that felt natural, not like a marketing tool. And in the world of modern music, sex appeal is the most powerful marketing tool there is, all-important and all-pervasive, particularly for female artists. Look at some of the best selling artists of 2006, the year Paramore were on the Warped Tour for the second time. Nelly Furtado's 'Promiscuous' spent six weeks at Number 1 on the *Billboard* 100, and features Nelly in a dialogue with Timbaland about the chances of his getting her in the sack. In July Justin Timberlake assured us he was going to bring 'SexyBack', and just to prove the point, he had a host of scantily clad women parading around in the video. Despite it being recorded for the Pink Panther movie, Beyonce's 'Check Up On It' seemed to be about tempting a man into a sexual encounter, rather than for a clumsy, moustachioed French detective. The Pussy Cat Dolls were informing Snoop Dog he was pushing their buttons, LL Cool J was telling Jennifer Lopez that he couldn't control himself, and the Black Eyed Peas' Fergie was insisting that she was, in fact,

Hayley working the crowd.

'Fergilicious'. Just a few months later, even Avril Lavgine would be stealing boyfriends and engaging in synchronised dance routines for her single 'Boyfriend', which would become her first Number 1 in the US.

Of course, all this is in danger of sounding puritanical. People fought for decades for the right to express their sexuality, be they male or female. Long may they continue to do so, especially in music videos, where it can also have the practical function of helping to sell records. But if you are a young girl or boy not yet comfortable with sex, or even an adult, or for that matter just a person who doesn't have much interest in the hyper-unreal, flawless sexual ideal offered by music videos then there aren't that many successful female artists to look to. Hayley offers an alternative. She proves that you can be a young attractive female in the music industry and not use your body to sell your music. As she says on *Absolutepunk.net*, "Just because I have boobs [some websites] have a couple more threads about Paramore... we make music for people to enjoy music, not so people can talk about my sexuality."

Hayley has been quite outspoken on the subject of feminine dignity on Paramore's LiveJournal. In one entry, she denounces skimpy female outfits on Halloween and in another she describes her disappointment, while at a stop-off in Las Vegas, at the amount of porn littering the streets in the appropriately named Sin City. Hayley has always been conscious of the tag of 'role model', fearing that it puts responsibility on her to appear perfect all the time. But all the same, with her outspoken views and emphasis on Paramore's music rather than her own appearance, a lot of people regard her as someone worthy of admiration. This is a fact she is quite comfortable with. "We've got a ton of girl fans, and it's rad being someone they can look up to," she told *Blender* in February 2008. "It's nice to show them that sex doesn't have to be all MTV'd out."

Back on the road, the Warped Tour was nearly over, and Paramore were well and truly on the way to success. Hayley had taken part in a photoshoot for *Kerrang!*, and would grace the front cover of the August 2006 issue along with Will Francis of horror-punks Aiden and Sonny Moore of post-hardcore Floridians From First To Last. It was part of a Warped Tour special, and the message was clear – Paramore had risen from side stage to contenders to full-on main stage conquerors over the course of the jaunt. *All We Know Is Falling* and *The Summer Tic* EP had been flying from the merchandise booth. Kevin

Lyman would go on to remember Paramore as one of the bands he saw blow up right before his eyes over the course of one Warped Tour. And just as an indication of how fast Paramore were picking up fans, Hayley Williams had been on the cover of one of the most widely read alternative music magazines [this *Kerrang!* Warped issue] before Paramore had even done a headline tour.

After a couple of days resting at home in Franklin following the completion of the Warped Tour, the band began rehearsing for their first ever headline tour. The American leg would begin on the August 2 and end on September 30, and as if any more evidence was needed that Paramore were well and truly making waves, all but five nights of the tour ultimately sold out. Since the Warped dates, Paramore had (finally) acquired a bus to tour in – they were no longer slumming it in a van, which afforded them simple luxuries like not having to stop to go to the toilet. It wasn't the absolute superstar lifestyle, however, as the bus did leak under heavy rainfall. The tour began in Chicago, Illinois, and passed through Ohio, Canada, Conneticut, West Virginia, New York, Michigan, Massachusetts, New Jersey, North Carolina, Maryland, Pennsylvania, Washington, California, Virginia, Rhode Island, Oregon, Utah, Colorado, Texas, Florida, Arizona, Kansas, Georgia, and ended up in Nasville, Tennessee. It took in no less than 23 states of America, spread over 36 dates – at first, it was meant to be even more.

After the Philadelphia date on August 20, Hayley's voice once again caved in due to the extreme demands and the band were forced to postpone a few shows and take a week off while she healed. The band posted an apology on their LiveJournal before picking up the tour once again in Seattle. Paramore went on the road with two other Fueled By Ramen acts – Cute Is What We Aim For and This Providence – and Hit The Lights, a pop punk quintet from Ohio.

One of the benefits of travelling in a bus meant that the band could begin writing material for the follow up to *All We Know Is Falling* while in transit. Josh had been, in Hayley's own words, "writing up a storm", throwing out riffs and guitar lines left, right and centre for Hayley to work with. But Hayley was struggling to actually get anything productive from these early writing sessions, even though she was really impressed by the material Josh was coming up with. She posted a message on their LiveJournal about the frustrations of writer's block, stating that although there were plenty of things that she felt she had to say, she was struggling to find the right words to say them.

By the time the tour came to an end, Paramore hailed it as the most fun they had ever had on the road. They had also confirmed that David Bendeth would be producing their second album, and that they would be heading into the studio to begin working on it as soon as they returned from their next appointment – a headline UK tour. It was only their second trip over the Atlantic, but the response in the UK was even more rapturous than the first time they had played. This time it was just Cute Is What We Aim For in the support slot, but once again, they managed to sell out all of the shows except for one. The UK headline tour ended in London at the Mean Fiddler, a sold-out show which also marked the end of the *All We Know Is Falling* chapter of Paramore's career.

The band were gearing up in earnest for their second album, and they had high hopes for it. Even whilst still touring for *All We Know Is Falling*, Hayley was anticipating the success of their as-yet-unrecorded follow-up. She told *Kerrang!* in 2006, "I think we're really going to make our mark with the album we're set to record in the winter." They hadn't had much of a rest since the release of *All We Know Is Falling*, but now that the touring of that record had finished, they took a month 'off', albeit to properly immerse themselves in rehearsing and writing a worthy follow-up. To facilitate the recording and distribution of the second album, the band had decided to team up with major label Atlantic Records, in tandem with the deal they had with Fueled By Ramen. The band has never expressed any dissatisfaction with FBR, which remains their de facto label. But there is no doubt that the kind of influence, contacts and financial support a label the size of Atlantic could offer would be a huge benefit to the band. Typically, however, bands that flirt with punk, even if just in terms of style and sound rather than ethos, are not looked upon favourably if they decided to take major label backing. This was not something that ever concerned Paramore: "We are not worried about people calling us sell-outs at all," Hayley insists. "I want everyone to be able to hear us." The band ultimately signed what is known as a '360' deal, something that has mainly come about since the rise of file sharing and the internet weakened a label's grasp of the distribution of their artists' music. Since this change in the environment, labels have typically been more reluctant to invest money in the development and promotion of artists, as they are not always guaranteed a good return on this investment. A 360 deal is where the label commits more money to all areas of an artist's development, from recording right the way through to promotion and touring, but in exchange they get a share of all profits that are associated with the band – not just album and single sales, but also things like ticket and merchandise sales. While this decision may have earned Paramore a few detractors, the band had always been completely open about their ambitions for success. Very early in their career they had made plain the fact that they wanted their band to be huge. "Our goal is to be where U2 are," Hayley said. "When you are a kid, you're not afraid to dream big, we just want to dream those dreams and not let reality stand in the way of achieving them."

chapter 7

THE *RIOT!* ACT

In December of 2006, the band went to meet with David Bendeth, the producer of the new record. They had met other producers prior to settling on David: Neal Avron, who had worked with New Found Glory and Fall Out Boy, and Howard Besnon, who had been at the desk for My Chemical Romance's *Three Cheers For Sweet Revenge*, among a host of others. Bendeth was not necessarily the obvious choice for Paramore. He had typically worked with heavier artists: metalcore acts like Killswitch Engage and Underoath, and melodic alternative metallers Breaking Benjamin. But Paramore insisted that Bendeth's passion and dedication was a draw for them. They were aware that there was a chance, based on the bands he tended to work with, that he wouldn't fit in "stylistically" with the band. But as Hayley remembers, he was incredibly eager to do the record. Hayley remembers him telling the band: "I love your sound. I want to do this record. I know this is going to be a challenge to make. I want to take on that challenge." And the fact that Bendeth had not worked with many bands that tend to be associated sonically with Paramore did not deter them. Hayley states that she loves the records that he'd produced with As I Lay Dying and Killswitch Engage, and that working with the likes of jazz-folk-blues artist Bruce Hornsby and late 1990s pop-rockers Vertical Horizon was a perfect demonstration of his versatility. "I always felt like we were a versatile band, but we didn't get to show that on our first record," Hayley mused to *AMP* magazine's John B Moore. "We needed someone like him to ring out that part of us and give us that confidence."

The majority of the writing for the album, aside from what had been done on tour, was completed when they got home from the UK dates at the end of 2006. Hayley had still been suffering from writer's block, perhaps attributable to "second album syndrome" – the pressure of producing a

Classic *Riot!* era.

superior follow-up to a successful debut often chokes an artist's creativity. As soon as she returned home to Franklin, she found that a complex mixture of emotions started to pour out of her. On the band's LiveJournal she divulged that she had hoped the experience of touring and being in a successful band would put to bed any other problems and hang-ups she had in her life. Returning from a year of solid gigging, she said that the whole band were on a high, and she thought that this feeling would continue once she came home. However, upon returning she realised that this was not the case, and that all of the things she had previously tried to hide, ignore or forget were still as present as ever. Fortunately, these dormant feelings would be the inspiration for the new songs. In one disarmingly vulnerable post, she revealed she felt ashamed of the feelings she was experiencing, such as hate, jealousy, lust, fear and pride. The experience of returning to all the same human drama that she had left in 2005 had a profound impact on Hayley and the writing of the record. She felt that she could no longer dismiss these feelings; they had to be dealt with, and this opened up a "deeper, darker, more vulnerable side" lyrically. As she later told *Kerrang!*, "It's basically OK to have scars and to show them." This newfound honesty would be the main source of inspiration for Hayley whilst writing lyrics for the record.

Another main development for the band as a whole was that the sheer workload of constant touring had sharpened everyone, changing them from an ambitious young teen band to professional, hard-working musicians. Hayley certainly noticed a change in the way that Josh played, stating in an interview that the new material he was writing was rawer, more memorable, and more aggressive than anything he'd come up with before. It was the perfect counterpart to Hayley's new mindset; she was determined not to "sugar coat" anything, as she had felt in the past, and Josh's new material had "a lot of really raw emotion in it" to complement the boldness of the lyrics.

As the new material began to come together, events were looking like they might all go very smoothly for Paramore. But just as was the case for *All We Know Is Falling*, a last minute line-up change would add plenty of drama to proceedings. It is not clear exactly when it happened – the band chose not to break the news until April of 2007, no doubt so that rumours and media attention would not distract from the recording of the album – but what is clear is that Hunter Lamb, who was brought in to replace Jason Bynum on guitar, did not go into the recording studio with Paramore. Announced as a band statement via the band's LiveJournal, an entry dated March 12, 2007, reads: "We have parted ways with our friend and guitarist for the past year, Hunter Lamb. We wish Hunter the best in all that he does next and in his engagement and marriage. It was a blessing getting to know him on the road and we were lucky to have him in the band with us… Sometimes, things just don't work out the way you thought they would." Though initial details of his departure were sketchy, more information began to emerge after the release. The main source of tension in the band, it seems, was Hunter's impending marriage. Josh told *Alternative Press* that "Hunter is getting married in the Fall and we totally support him, but we were all a little sceptical about how he would maintain a marriage and stay totally focused on the band." Later, Hayley would expand on this, saying that Hunter's engagement was not the only reason that the band felt he was no longer the right guitarist for them. "Some of it had to do with his playing," she said in *NME*, "and a lot of it had to do with feeling like none of us were on the same page as him in the band." But though Hunter was no longer a part of the Paramore fold, they say that the band and Hunter are still on good terms. "I guess we have a curse!" Josh would ponder.

Once the majority of the second record was written, the band moved to New Jersey to be nearer David Bendeth's studio, House of Loud, in Elmwood Park, where the album would be recorded. The band have stated that the experience of moving away from home and living in a hotel together, being isolated from their friends and family, was an important bonding experience, and one that had a positive impact on their work for the record. The most pressing issue after Hunter's departure was how to continue with only one guitarist. Paramore were happy for the time being as a four-piece, but they wanted to maintain the depth and melodic variety that having more than one guitar part gives. In the end, it was decided that Josh would record all of the guitar parts himself, meaning that he essentially had double the workload. "To teach someone the guitar part and them have them execute it the way that I saw it in my head would be a little more difficult than [for] me to just go ahead and play it myself," Josh said to the *Artisan News Service*.

Unlike their first album, which was recorded in three weeks, the band had a full three months to record the follow-up. This meant that their entire approach to recording could change. They now had the opportunity to dwell on the songs a little more, develop them and pick apart songs at will until they were totally satisfied. The relaxed time scale also gave Hayley a chance to experiment more with the vocal melodies. It is something that she wished she had been able to do on the more rushed *All We Know Is Falling*. For the second album the vocal textures would be much more dense and complex. Despite having plenty of time, David Bendeth was a constant source of motivation, pushing the band hard to get the most out of them. Every song had to be bang on tempo, which required multiple takes of the same track. Josh remembers that as the main time keeper, this was particularly hard on Zac, but David Bendeth would later hail Zac as a "monster" behind the drum set.

During the recording, Paramore also ran a competition through their official website, offering fans the chance to sing on the track 'Born For This'. The competition was called 'The Last Song You Will Ever Sing', and to enter fans had to upload a video of themselves singing a Paramore song for the opportunity to sing the gang vocals on the track. The winner was one Mary Bonney, from Virginia, who gave a spirited rendition of 'Woah' for Paramore's viewing pleasure, which can be found on YouTube. Along with a few runners-up, she went to meet the band at House of Loud, where in exchange for their contribution to the record, they were treated to a tour of the studio, a one-on-one drum lesson from Zac, and some southern hospitality from Jeremy and Josh who manned the barbeque. Mary gave the author a fascinating insight into the band's world from a fan's perspective. Her initial reaction upon hearing that she had won was, "Disbelief... I was just completely floored," she said. "The President of Atlantic Records called my cell and told me, and I couldn't stop screaming 'Oh my God!' after he hung up. It was surreal, knowing that I was going to meet Paramore. Singing on the record didn't even register with me – just knowing that I was going to meet them was enough to make me flip." She described the atmosphere in the studio as "very laid-back", stating that "everyone was hanging out like friends, and they had arcade games, video games, tons of junk food. There were couches, a kitchen... it was almost like a home." Mary is slightly older than Hayley, and given how relaxed everyone was in the studio, it makes you wonder what the interactions were like between fan and band. "They actually seemed my age!" Mary reveals. "It was weird at first since I'm older than most of them, yet I was so nervous about meeting them. But they were so down-to-earth and willing to talk about anything and everything. Hayley and I talked about clothing, make-up, hair… but we also talked about vocal health and the pressures of gaining fame too quickly. They seemed to have a great balance of maturity but also knew how to kick back and grill some awesome burgers."

'The Last Song You Will Ever Sing' competition was clearly a gift to the fans, and Mary has some interesting ideas about why Paramore has such a devoted fanbase. "I think they have a connection because they slowly gained fame, so they got to really connect and meet fans from the beginning (like during tours for *All We Know Is Falling*). I think that made them really appreciate the support we give them and they don't want to lose that, no matter how big they get. They had the YouTube contest because they wanted fans to be involved with the new record, and they wanted to show the fans that they wanted to sort of… give back to us. Even if people didn't win the contest, just knowing Paramore still cared about them was enough." After her experience of meeting the band, Mary couldn't disagree more with the old adage 'never meet your heroes.' "Man, I wouldn't say that at all!" she said. "Meeting Paramore was the highlight of my life and only made me like and respect them even more. Usually you build your favourite artist up so much that when you meet them, they are inevitably not what you hoped for, but Paramore were so great. I couldn't have asked for a better experience and it was so great getting to know them for the awesome people they are." There is no doubt at all in Mary when she says, "They deserve all the success in the world."

The day of the competition wasn't the only time Paramore took to have a little fun, though. They definitely took the phrase 'work hard, play hard' to heart, and found some interesting ways to blow off steam whilst they weren't in the studio. When asked what they did to pass the time, they revealed a rather destructive side to themselves. "The engineers that work at Bendeth's studio are amazing," Josh says. "They're such cool dudes. There's this one guy who likes to blow up stuff. He builds little sticks of dynamite." Out in the parking lot a cake, an acoustic guitar and even a toilet fell prey to the engineer's and the band's appetite for destruction.

Perhaps appropriately, they decided to call the album *Riot!*, though it's not really anything to do with blowing up toilets. In fact, it's nothing to do with violence at all, but rather the unchecked, passionate force of the album, as Hayley explained on the *www.paramore.net* official band bio at the time:

"For us, the title literally means an unbridled outburst of emotions. When we were writing, it seemed like our thoughts and emotions were coming out so fast that we couldn't control them. It felt like there was a riot within us. So the album takes our passion to a new level; it's just all raw energy."

The phrase 'raw energy' could be a description of the second album's impassioned opener, 'For A Pessimist, I'm Pretty Optimistic'. Kicking straight in with what the Farro brothers do best – a massive, melodic riff and powerhouse drumming – it contains all the elements that a Paramore fan would recognise from *All We Know Is Falling*, but with something new, something quite difficult to pin down. It's not the huge hooks or anthemic chorus – they were there before – but it's the way they're delivered, with an absolute conviction and confidence that belies the band's youth. It embodies what the rest of the album achieves so well, which is the absolute synthesis of Paramore's pop and rock elements. Whereas *All We Know Is Falling* sounded like a rock band with an ear for a great melody, 'For a Pessimist...' shows a rock band who can write great songs, absolutely in control of all their precocious talent and channelling it into a three-minute thrill ride. The lyrics discuss the disappointment of having someone you trusted let you down, and it does demonstrate a new, more honest approach to songwriting from Hayley. There's more jagged emotion in the words, yes, but the words are better too; there's less cliché, and more of a young woman finding her voice.

After 'For A Pessimist, I'm Pretty Optimistic', the album launches straight into 'That's What You Get', which is not just the finest song on the album, but the finest song the band had written up to this point. It's nothing short of a masterpiece, the kind of song that manages to be strong, melancholy, frustrated and triumphant, all whilst making you want to jump up and down in a concert hall with a thousand other people. Every section of the song is tailor-made to affect the listener, and it all fits together with a kind of bespoke simplicity. Skipping along on a slightly off-beat groove, every line that Hayley sings is like a tuneful bullet that will bury itself in your brain for weeks. Bendeth's production shines, too, allowing the rhythm to drive the song forward in the verse and pre-chorus and giving Hayley's vocal the room to soar in the chorus. The overlapping vocal harmonies in the breakdown are beautifully heartfelt, matching the plaintive longing of the lyrics, but when some shouty gang vocals crash in, they don't sound out of place at all.

Hayley's lyrics sound like a woman who has outgrown teenage angst histrionics, and is now a little wiser and more world-weary. The song is a triumph from beginning to end.

Future single 'Hallelujah' takes its foot off the gas a little, less driving and insistent than it's two predecessors. But it's just as immediate, and nothing short of epic in scope. It shows a band with real courage and self-confidence to look outside of their melodic punk-rock roots and write a song that sounds like it should be played in an arena to tens of thousands of people; a band that aren't afraid to strive for world domination. The chord changes are big and bold, and Hayley's vocal gymnastics are stretched to their absolute limit. The chorus is rallying and uplifting, but Paramore once again pull off the coup of underpinning the whole affair with a real despondence, preventing it from turning into a mindless, punch-the-air exercise. The lyrical content is actually deceptively dark, as Hayley explained in *Kerrang!*: 'Hallelujah' is about facing chaos and going through a lot of terrible things in your life but then being able to stand there and say, 'I'm going to make it through this, I'm going straight through and I'll come out the other end really strong.'" The song is actually one of the most challenging on the album to record. The acoustic version that already existed on the early bootleg had been in circulation among fans for some time. Hayley personally felt an immense amount of pressure to top this version and was concerned that fans had become accustomed to it and would not take to the new re-working. But this concern made her push herself even harder to make the song all it could be, putting every ounce of emotion she could muster into it, and she was ultimately delighted with the outcome.

Track four is the song that would really launch Paramore into superstardom, and for many, the outstanding song on the album: 'Misery Business'. The muffled string intro lasts just a few seconds, and there's no containing what comes after. It is a raucous, hook-laden, blistering melée of buzz-saw guitars and yelped vocals, as breathtaking a slice of furious pop-punk as you could hope to hear. The guitar lines are jagged and the pounding drums almost stutter in the frantic verse, while Hayley half-sings, half-talks about a manipulative girl who took someone from her, and her satisfaction at reclaiming him. She demonstrates a real mean streak in her lyrics, cutting and scathing, with no hint of remorse. It's an as-yet-unseen side to her, and it's got sass and swagger by the bucket-load. All the faltering rhythms stop in the chorus, however, which is undeniable in its simplicity and power. But for all its attitude on record, it was a difficult song for Hayley to write. As she explained, "Misery business is probably the most shameful and anger-filled song on the record." She also states that the actual situation was far darker than the fictionalised one heard on record, in which she "made myself come off a lot stronger than I was at the time." In a LiveJournal post written after the release of the album, she revealed the story behind the song. She states that it is about a girl who used sex and her body to manipulate a close friend of Hayley's – to the point where no one could recognise him. Her thinking she was in love with this particular boy intensified the anger Hayley felt. 'Misery Business' represents her finally addressing those suppressed feelings, and it has had a cathartic effect for her. "It's a pretty embarrassing situation," she said in *Alternative Press*, "and it took me a long time to feel strong enough to say something about it. But now, three years later, I'm no longer reliving it." And, just to conclude the real life version of the tale, the errant boy in question finally realised the error of his ways and broke up with his seductress in favour of Hayley.

Unfortunately, after 'Misery Business' comes the first faltering moment of the record. 'When It Rains' is really Paramore's first stab at a ballad proper.

It's not a total catastrophe, or even particularly bad for that matter – but after the relentlessly brilliant opening of the record, it feels out of place. It really draws to the fore the hint of 1980s influence that you can hear throughout the record, a sort of New Romantic synth-pop cuteness transposed to 21st Century rock. There are nice melodies in abundance, in particular the genuinely beautiful vocal breakdown, but it feels pleasant rather than moving or affecting. The biggest concern about 'When It Rains', however, is that it completely lacks any of the bite that distinguishes Paramore from the crop of MOR pop-rockers which they have always managed to rise well above. Lyrically it's full of regret and sadness, and Hayley's vocal delivery is full of longing as she appeals to an unnamed addressee who is shutting themself away from her. But it perhaps lacks some of the self-awareness or maturity you can hear on other tracks on the album.

'Let The Flames Begin' goes some way to getting *Riot!* back on track, though it's not one of the strongest tunes on the record. It has a harder edge than the rest of the album, drawing from post-hardcore influences like Refused and mewithoutYou (who Hayley had been listening to a lot whilst recording *Riot!*), but put together in a simple verse-chorus, melodic package. A slicing guitar lead line accompanies Hayley's vocals in the chorus, which is one of the most angry and strident on the album, and begs to be blasted out of giant speakers at ear-bleed volume. The rest of the song drags a bit however, not feeling urgent enough to match the impassioned lyrics. That said, it would become a live favourite for the band, and understandably so: in a gig environment the bold, simple riffs really come to life.

The next two tracks are a real return to the form promised by the album's openers. 'Miracle' is a fairly straightforward emotional pop-punk tune, but the simple beauty of the guitar lines and the rhythm is devastatingly effective. Of course, the mercilessly catchy chorus doesn't hurt, which is as insistent and forceful as anything else on the record. It doesn't exactly reinvent the wheel, but every element is perfect: the choppy, palm-muted verse, the simple bass line, the tight rock drumming – it's not so much what they're doing, but the way they do it that sets them apart. Hayley's vocal is unsurprisingly brilliant, particularly in the verse, where she stretches her range and gives a performance very few other front-women – or men – can offer. Lyrically, it's plainly optimistic and uplifting in a way that the album hasn't yet tried to be, as Hayley sings of having faith in things getting better

and facing her demons. In a way it seems to address her writing of the album's lyrics; she sings of how it is time to stop hiding away her fears and hurt, and instead to start believing things will get better. The song crescendos to a huge final twenty seconds, and as the last chord is still ringing, three drum beats mark the introduction of 'crushcrushcrush'. This song flirts with electro-pop most blatantly of all the tracks on the album, and it has a kind of camp drama to it that makes it hard to take seriously. Not that this is a bad thing; the song has a few playful elements, like Hayley's whispering and Josh's shouting 'two three four!' in the breakdown, or the jaunty, dancy riff that is introduced after the first chorus. You get the impression that, above all, the song is supposed to be fun; and for all its dalliance with 1980s synth silliness, the rip-roaring rock chorus doesn't play around. It's great to hear Hayley sing of troublesome relationships with her tongue in her cheek a little, and you feel its something she'd never have attempted on *All We Know Is Falling*. The middle-eight flies a bit close to the sun, however, and Hayley's rallying cry of 'rock and roll, baby…' calls to mind Britney Spears more than Joan Jett. Other than that, though, it's one of the stand-out moments on the album, and the first time Paramore have played around with their formula and come off better for it.

The opposite of which is true for 'We Are Broken'. Opening with a haunting synth drone, some programmed drums and minor piano chords back Hayley's low, melancholy lines in the verse. So far, so bearable. But as a big drum fill ushers in the chorus, you realise you're dealing with a ballad more suited to a Broadway musical than the 21st Century's most promising rock upstarts. It's the same problem that Paramore seemed to have on 'When It Rains'; they know how to write a good ballad melody but they can't yet seem to do it full justice with an interesting arrangement. The chilling, atmospheric opening promises something far more challenging than what is ultimately delivered. The lyrics, according to Hayley, are about looking at a world that seems to be desperately reaching out for some kind of hope but finding none – you get the impression that if Hayley had stuck more plainly to personal experience, as she does on the rest of the album, the outcome would've been more affecting. As it stands, 'We Are Broken' is the weakest song on the album. Even the introduction of an organ in the final seconds, suggesting some kind of divine hope, can't save it.

The penultimate track, 'Fences', is a tricky one. It's an exuberant indie-rock track, which skips along on a snare beat and restless bass line. Hayley's excitable vocal delivery in the verses is full of panache and witty lyricisms, and has a clear Berlin-style cabaret influence, matching the themes of faded glamour and the pressure of being in the limelight. Considering

'Fences' is the most playful track Paramore had ever written, it's pulled off with an absolute precision and confidence, and like 'crushcrushcrush', it's one of the lighter and more fun moments on the album. It sounds remarkably like their fellow talented youngsters and label mates Panic! At The Disco – particularly their song 'But It's Better If You Do', which was released as a single in 2006. Nonetheless, it's good to hear Paramore trying out a few new ideas and expanding the scope of their sound.

The final track is the incendiary 'Born For This', a track tailor-made to ignite live shows. Opening with a slab of punk-rock riffery as stirring as anything on the record, the verse is a boisterous combination of twitchy guitar work, assertive rhythms and rousing gang vocals. A chugging guitar and bass line pins the song to earth as Hayley's vocal takes off in the chorus, and the message is clear: it's a love song, a thank you note, and a call to arms for all of Paramore's fans. In the pre-chorus, Hayley's chant is "we want the airwaves back," a line taken from 'Liberation Frequency' by Swedish post-punkers Refused. It's a smart and interesting inclusion: it's a nod to a hugely influential and important band, and a statement of intent for Paramore as they embark on the next stage of their career. As Hayley explains, "This is our introduction to radio… and I guess 'we want the airwaves back' is a really ballsy line because we've never been on the radio before. I kind of took it out of their song and fit it in – 'our fans are going to carry us to the next level' – we're going to be introduced to all these new people who have never heard of us and we're going to take over." The song was written in January, in pre-production, just before the band went into the studio. At this time Hayley was deeply concerned about the state of the album, wondering on the LiveJournal if they yet had anything like the material they desired. Hayley went back to her hotel room and starting browsing the community (the forums that are accessible through Paramore's LiveJournal) and found herself inspired by the dedication and support of their fans. She began writing down some lyrics, and two hours later, 'Born For This' was written. It's a powerful and fitting close to *Riot!*, an album which maintains and expands upon Paramore's beginnings in *All We Know Is Falling* but clearly has its eyes set on mainstream takeover.

Riot! is, in short, a great album. Hayley's voice is remarkable throughout, and Josh's guitar lines seem all the stronger and more direct for him recording them all himself. The rhythm section, driven by Zac's absolute conviction and power behind the kit and backed up by Jeremy's simple and effective bass playing, is the engine room for the entire album, which rattles along at real pace. The record is at its strongest when Paramore build upon what they already know, developing into a better version of what they were before. Tracks like 'That's What You Get', 'Misery Business' and 'Born For This' show the same grasp of emotional, melodic pop-punk rock, but are assembled in a way that is infinitely more confident and self-assured. They demonstrate a band that in around eighteen months had taken a huge leap forward in the development of their sound. But where *Riot!* falls short is when the band tries to move beyond territory that they had already explored. The soft-rock styling of 'When It Rains' and melodramatic balladry of 'We Are Broken' show the band trying to expand their sound, but struggling to find their own voice. There's just nothing remarkable about those songs; none of that intangible magic that usually sets Paramore apart. However, these black spots aside, there is no doubt that *Riot!* was a huge step forward from *All We Know Is Falling*. Paramore had graduated from contenders to full-blown rock stars, and they knew it. They stated numerous times that this was the album that they were really proud of, and the one that, if the band were to split up the day after, they would want to be remembered for. As Hayley says: "I feel that this record, compared to the last, is much more fearless… This record isn't safe at all. I feel like this record's going to show people who we really are."

Unfortunately, not all of the music media were in agreement. *Kerrang!* were marginally less scathing about *Riot!* than they had been about *All We Know Is Falling*: where *AWKIF* had been "precisely the sound of style dancing on substance's grave," they said that the main issue with *Riot!* was "retracing old steps, playing it safe and unswervingly sticking to the same old rigid formula," which seems to deny the absolute honing of the sound evident. They gave the album three K's, however, denoting it as "good". *NME* disagreed, saying that it was the band's attempts to expand their sound that had been their undoing. "Witness 'When It Rains'," the reviewer writes, "a 'slowie' that by dint of its sonic perfection ends up sounding like 1980s power-balladeers Heart." Another gripe was that Bendeth's production was too slick, ironing out "every crease with a very expensive iron." Other publications were more positive: *Alternative Press* thought that the album "fell a few steps short of front-runner status in the nu-emo genre," but praised Hayley's "never phoned in" vocal talents and the "mightily impressive" musicianship of the rest of the band, ultimately giving the album three stars our of five. Popular website *Allmusic.com* praised the honesty of Hayley's lyrics, saying that they "feel authentic and representative of actual teenage puppy love, where a break-up feels like the end of the world." They also felt that the slower songs on offer were some of the strongest moments on the album, displaying the band's "maturity as musicians." Unfortunately, they couldn't quite resist the seemingly obvious Avril Lavgine comparison, though they did note Hayley's superior voice and that "her image isn't manufactured to be rebellious and angst-ridden." *Absolutepunk.net* followed up its positive review of their debut with a similar cautious caveat: "Call it a 'guilty pleasure' if you must," writes reviewer Jason Tate, "but I'm relatively certain many of you will have a similar reaction upon hearing this album in full, maybe something like: 'Fuck, I can't believe I actually like this.'"

The response to *Riot!* had not really won over the hearts of the music media. Despite the huge leap that Paramore had made, their status remained that of a band who inspired huge devotion from fans, yet something like mild distaste from journalists. But the music press does not always dictate a band's popularity or success, and sometimes, the fans carry a band above how they are perceived in the media. As Paramore were about to prove.

chapter 8

GRACE

To support the release of *Riot!*, 'Misery Business' was chosen as the lead single. It was launched on July 10 with a promo shot by Shane Drake in LA. It features a performance in a room where 'Riot!' is scrawled all over in the same style as the album artwork. The band are sporting the new style which they would stick with throughout the *Riot!* campaign: bright, bold contrasts of red, yellow and black. The narrative of the video concerns a high-school she-devil who patrols the corridors generally spreading misery: cutting off ponytails, abusing sensitive, willowy boys, and kissing other people's boyfriends. She is the classroom tyrant who Paramore barely had time to experience in their short school careers. However, they knock her down a peg or too anyway, Hayley unceremoniously stripping her of her chicken fillets and make-up. It's a clear adaptation of the song's lyrical content, and a perfect platform for the band to launch *Riot!*, but the key to the video is actually the performance segments. For many people this was their first glimpse of Paramore, and the band make it a memorable one. Paradoxically Hayley almost embodies the girl she sings of as she struts and shimmies her way through the performance, fire-red hair flailing around her tiny frame. Zac's drumming looks as commanding as it sounds, and Josh and Jeremy throw their instruments around with a force bordering on disdain. They'd always looked good in front of the camera, but now they looked like they knew it.

The single came in various formats, with numerous B-sides and rarities for fans to enjoy. The US single came with 'Stop This Song (Love Sick Melody)', a track recorded during the *Riot!* sessions. Hayley remarked that it was her favourite song to record in the studio, as the vocal breakdown contains around seventy tracks all overlapping. She recalled a studio engineer asking her, "'Are we done? Do you wanna add anything else?' and I'd be like

'Yeah!'" It's a moody, fast-paced track with a wrenching verse and indignant chorus, and the bridge in question is an impressive demonstration of Hayley's ear for vocal harmonies. Other versions came with an acoustic cover of the Foo Fighters' magnificent 'My Hero', from their 1997 album *The*

Paramore with guitarist Taylor York.

Colour And The Shape. Paramore's version was initially recorded for the *Sound of Superman* accompaniment to the 2006 film *Superman Returns*, and features various other acts that they had toured or played with, including Plain White T's, The Receiving End Of Sirens and The Academy Is… Hayley's voice carries the subdued acoustic version very nicely. One vinyl version of the single came with a rather interesting B-side: a cover of U2's 'Sunday Bloody Sunday', which first appeared on the Irish supergroup's 1983 album *War*. It's rather odd to hear a teen American band singing of the Bloody Sunday Massacre that happened thousands of miles away in 1970s Northern Ireland. They've stripped the song of a lot of its indignation, slowing it down and giving it an acoustic work over, to the point where it has more in common with Incubus' surf-indie hit 'Drive' than the original.

With the help of the 'Misery Business' promo, *Riot!* had a successful opening week, selling 42,000 copies. It wasn't a monumental beginning, but three more singles and constant touring would raise their profile such that the album would continually pick up pace, peaking at Number 15 on the *Billboard* Hot 100 some three months after its release. Similarly, 'Misery Business' had a relatively slow start, entering the charts at Number 99. But as word began to spread, sales of the single would continue to climb, and it was certified platinum in September, signifying over one million sales.

Not everyone was a huge fan of the single. It had come under fire from some quarters for the use of the word 'God' as an exclamation in the song; a minor infraction, it might seem, except that the band had always been open about their faith. Coming from a deeply religious part of the country, and professing their faith in interviews, there was perhaps an expectation that they would present themselves as role models or ambassadors for the Christian community. The use of God's name in this way ran counter to these hopes. On the other side of the coin, some had accused the content of the song as being preachy and puritanical, mainly because of the use of the word 'whore' in the song. Hayley was trapped between a rock and a hard place. The band had always been cautious of the label of 'Christian band' as Josh stated in an interview, "We are Christian, but we're not a Christian band. We're just like everyone else, you know? We have our own beliefs." The questions that naturally arise from this assertion are these – what is the difference between a band of Christians and a Christian band? And aren't the tenets of rock 'n' roll at odds with the tenets of organised religion?

One estemmed researcher at a British university who is studying the relationship between punk rock and Christianity for a doctorate, doesn't think so (his name is withheld here by request). A large number of bands from the southern states of the US are outspoken Christians: there seems a particular relationship between hardcore/metalcore, with bands like Norma Jean, The Chariot and Underoath, and the faith. When asked by the author about this relationship, the researcher revealed: "The question of why so many Christians in the USA are drawn to hardcore kinda misses the point. They are drawn to every conceivable style of popular and unpopular music… everything from twee 1970s folk to ambient techno to cheesy electro-pop to industrial music to death metal. I can tell you with some degree of confidence that the only genre of popular culture that Christianity has not employed is pornography."

The origins of Contemporary Christian Music, or CCM as it is known,

are complex, as the researcher explains: "CCM basically developed from within the Jesus Movement, which was the Christian faction of the hippy-led counterculture of the 1960s and 1970s. When the hippies arrived en masse in San Francisco, there were a number of diverse Christian churches and communes waiting for them. The Jesus Movement adopted the culture of the counterculture, including the music." It is here that Christianity's relationship with punk was first engendered, a relationship which exists to this day. In the realm of punk, the on-going significance of the Jesus Movement is that one of its constituent members, the Chicago-based Jesus People USA are still around, living in a big commune and organising the annual Cornerstone Festival that features many Christian punk, hardcore and metal bands [basically a Christian Woodstock]. If a Christian punk/metal band plays Cornerstone, they got a real shot at making a career of it." Paramore had played the Cornerstone Festival in 2005, one of their first festival appearances before getting signed.

So if Christianity and punk rock aren't necessarily uneasy bedfellows, then what is the distinction between a 'Christian band' and a 'band of Christians'? The researcher explains the distinction, referencing Paramore's friendship with and respect for bands like Underoath, Norma Jean and The Chariot. "It's not surprising in one sense," he says, "since these are some of the major 'cross-over' Christian metalcore bands. Like Paramore and various other, less commercially successful bands, they're Christians accepted and embraced by Christians and non-Christians alike. It has been a concern of some bands full of Christians that 'coming out', so to speak, would wreck their commercial opportunities… At the same time there have been examples of artists who emerged in the Christian music industry who went mainstream and were abandoned by their Christian fans, assuming that by switching genres they'd given up their religion. So, Norma Jean, Underoath and the Chariot are able to exist as what are called by some in the CCM industry 'tweener' bands – their fanbase and their identity is shared between the CCM market and mainstream genre market. It's understandable, then, that they would be role models for Paramore." One of the major developments in this kind of cross-over appeal was the formation of a pivotal record label, as the researcher elucidates. "The most significant development in Christian punk/hardcore was the emergence of Tooth & Nail Records in the mid-1990s, in Seattle… they developed a market for the 'tweener' bands. For example MxPx and Anberlin started out on T&N, two bands with a strong sense of antipathy towards the CCM industry at large. An interview with T&N founder Brendan Ebel a few years back quoted him stating with pride that half T&N's sales came from Christian book/music stores and half from mainstream record stores."

Over the years, Paramore have played with a large number of current or former Tooth & Nail bands: Anberlin, mewithoutYou, Underoath, Norma Jean and of course Copeland, with whom they played their first ever gig. It is easy to see why these sort of bands would provide useful models for Paramore. "[It would help] to have these sorts of bands and labels around the place that they can use as role models and examples of the idea that they wouldn't have to hide their beliefs in the mainstream, but nor would they have to preach in order to feel that they were still being true to living out their faith. In other words, there was a role for Christians in music other than as a praise and worship or explicitly evangelist, missionary band."

With this history in mind, a lot of Paramore's comments on their faith come into sharper focus. There is no attempt to mask their beliefs – in the past they have spoken about praying prior to playing a show, attending church and so on. In *Kerrang!*, Hayley spoke of the positive affect that faith has on her life: "Because of my belief in Jesus, I have hope in more things than I would if I didn't have that faith. And who wouldn't like more hope in their lives, regardless of whether it comes from Jesus or not?" But at the same time, the band make it clear that their music is not a vehicle for spreading a Christian message. They speak of their admiration for U2 and Jimmy Eat World, bands that use words like "faith" and "hope" in a more universal, general sense. "We try not to push our faith on anybody," Hayley says. "It's there because it's a part of us and people sense it."

With all this in mind, the 'Misery Business' controversy makes more sense. Paramore are caught between the two worlds they inhabit. On the one hand, some members of the Christian community regard them as not devout enough, and on the other, members of the secular community regard them with suspicion because of their faith. Hayley's response, however, is a testament to both her honesty and her diplomacy. She once again took to her LiveJournal to respond to the accusations. She admitted to taking God's name in vain in the song, but insisted that she didn't take the subject of her saviour lightly. Rather, she explains that it was her faith that helped her deal with the painful feelings she sings of in 'Misery Business', and that she is a different person now than when she first felt them. As for accusations that the song was puritanical, Hayley remarked that "a lot of things have been printed to make it sound that way because it's more interesting to read," and confirmed sex to be, in her eyes, "a beautiful thing."

By now the band had begun rehearsing for upcoming shows, and were well aware of the need to replace absent guitarist Hunter Lamb. They posted a message on their LiveJournal announcing who the replacement would be: "We should probably tell you that one of our good friends Taylor York is going to come and fill in as back-up guitar player for the next few tours. Hopefully he'll stay longer…" Born Taylor Benjamin York on December 17, 1989, the new guitarist had first met Josh and Zac at a vacation Bible school when he was eleven. Josh was wearing a Jimmy Eat World T-shirt, and Taylor was immediately eyeing the pair up as potential Bible buddies. But it was not until he transferred to their school that the friendship really took off; Taylor's older brother Justin played in a local band named Cecil Adora, and Taylor had his suspicions that the reflected glory was the main reason for Zac and Josh wanting to befriend him. Taylor went on to briefly play with Seraphim, the band Zac and Josh were in with school friend Randall Thomas; so he had been on the Paramore radar since its inception.

In April, Paramore embarked on their first tour since the previous October, and they made sure that this time they stepped things up a bit. Zac had started playing to a click track in an ear-piece to ensure that the band kept absolutely exact time. "In the beginning, we were hesitant," Hayley

The glamour of life on the road.

revealed in *Rock Sound*, "because it seemed too professional but if you want to be a good musician, then timing is a big part of it." Zac went even further to explain the reasons the band were hesitant to get too 'professional': "Part of us does want to be Muse live," he said, referring to the British alt-rock band that had earned a reputation for incredible live performances. "We do want to be solid, flawless, and perfect live. But a part of us wants to be Underoath or New Found Glory and make it raw and fun, going crazy and not caring if you mess up. We try to balance the two." The US tour began in Florida and ended one month later in California, passing through eleven other states and two stop-offs in Canada. "This is our first tour back on the road after finishing our record and the fans are just great," Hayley said, "better than ever really. We're seeing a lot of new kids come out to the shows; some of the same faces that we saw on the last tour and they're bringing friends out." When the band came through Orlando, they also stopped off at the Fort Studio (where they had previously recorded the second part of *All We Know Is Falling* with Mike Green). They booked a room for a day to rehearse and rearrange the set list a little. Hayley said that the band will always love Orlando "like a second home" – it was, after all, where their career really began to take shape. When the US tour ended they had just six days off before the European tour started in Paris, France, where they played with multi-platinum goth-rockers Evanescence. From there they headed over to the UK for a few dates, including a stint at the Ponty Pridd Festival in Wales, and then on to shows in Amsterdam, Vienna and Frankfurt. And with the buzz around *Riot!* steadily building, the press was beginning to take more and more notice of Paramore. A landmark moment came for them when they were given their first *Kerrang!* cover feature as a band. Yet even this was to prove something of a Trojan horse.

The issue was released at the end of May and the band must have been excited to see themselves staring out of one of the most widely read and long-running alternative music magazines. But even though the feature was the main attraction for that issue – given four pages and a full size picture – the article was not particularly what Paramore had expected. Instead, it focused on a number of aspects of the band's personalities and relationships which caught the writer's attention (the revered Tom Bryant). Chief amongst the most eyebrow-raising assertions were: Josh writing 'Riot!' on Hayley's T-shirt, touching her breasts "with an intimacy that suggests neither of them mind him touching her there"; Hayley being demanding; the suggestion that they didn't miss Hunter, or further still, were "almost glad he was gone"; that Hayley is "always vying for attention, but when she gets it, or if it challenges her, she doesn't quite know what to do with it"; and, that "Zac and Jeremy are forever twining their legs around one another's, sitting virtually on top of one another whenever possible." The tone of the article generally casts the band as uncomfortable adolescents headed up by an overbearing front-woman.

Paramore were understandably upset, as Hayley explained on LiveJournal, questioning if there was "one bit of truth" in it and ridiculing the comments about touching her breasts and the boys being her "bitches". She also expanded on the Hunter issue, asserting that while their relationship with Hunter was not the same as it had been, they still "love that dude to death."

Unpleasant experiences with the press aside, Paramore still had an album to promote and next on the agenda was their third stint on the Warped Tour. Since Paramore first began, this tour has seemed bound to them in some way, and doubtless many die-hard Paramore fans were won in the blistering heat of a Warped Tour stop-off. It is a fact the band knows well. As Josh told *USA Today*, "We owe Kevin Lyman our souls. He's basically given us everything we have." The set-up was familiar – a cross-country trek featuring about eighty bands over forty separate dates. Their set list would predominantly feature tracks from *Riot!*, though they did throw in the likes of 'Emergency', 'Pressure' and 'Here We Go Again', songs they'd been playing the previous year at Warped. This time, though, Paramore would not be battling for crowds on side stages; they were to be playing on the main stage, a fact which they acknowledged was a big responsibility. Joining them on the tour were plenty of friends and ex-tour mates: Anberlin, Bayside, Cute Is What We Aim For, My American Heart and Norma Jean, to name but a few. It must have been strange for the band to be once again touring with many of the acts they had previously supported, but now eclipsing them in terms of crowd sizes. Paramore were also touring with New Found Glory, and the band would become close friends with the Floridian pop-punk veterans.

Since the success of 'Misery Business', *Riot!* had been selling increasingly well, and this in turn put stress on the band in terms of workload. Signs of strain were beginning to show. Inititally the frustration was just at the sheer intensity of the Warped experience, as Zac explained: "Let me tell you the truth. Warped Tour is the most brutal tour ever... The kids are awesome and always so passionate, but the tour is brutal. You wake up and it's so hot, you go do press and it's so hot, and then you play and it's even hotter!" But the band was finding that the relentless pressure to promote their music and keep themselves in the public eye was wearing them down. Hayley remembers that this began to negatively effect the way the band were interacting with one another – tempers had begun to fray and they were regularly arguing with one another. On one occasion she even remembers Josh bursting into tears, such was his frustration and desperation to go home. "That's when we realised," she said in *Rock Sound*, "that we weren't really looking out for ourselves, we were just looking out for everyone else's interests."

But this is something that Kevin Lyman noticed too, and the band shared an anecdote which demonstrates that Lyman didn't just offer the band career opportunities – he offered them relief and friendship, too. Noticing that they were being pushed extremely hard, he had spoken to them, explaining that he had seen other acts get burned out so many times before, and it was crucial that they got time off to recharge. Perhaps seeing that they were struggling to find this free time, in July he took matters into his own hands and arranged for Paramore to have a 12p.m. slot – the earliest slot available (on the Warped Tour show times are not fixed, they rotate). He then spoke to Paramore's management and asked that they have no press that day, as immediately after their set, he would be taking them on a fishing expedition. They were taken to the coast were they boarded a boat, which took them out to the middle of the ocean. They spent the entire day fishing and relaxing, though some of the events on the boat would have been better left there: the band would later recount how Captain Dave cut the leg off a live octopus he had caught, and ate it raw in front of the shocked band. Not to be outdone, Taylor followed suit and sampled one of the legs too. The octopus was then thrown back into the water, "so it could have and live a happy life." Everyone also took the opportunity to take a swim, away from the thunderous press junket they had been in the midst of. "I guess," said Hayley, "Kevin really meant what he said when he told us he wanted us to relax." But even though it seems clear that the band sorely needed this chance to let off some steam – if you're eating raw octopus legs, you must be pretty wound up – it almost didn't happen. Such is the immense demand that pursues a successful band, some interviews had to be scheduled on the day of the trip anyway. Conducting these interviews held them up, and Lyman very nearly left for the open seas without them. This story serves as a powerful reminder of just how practically challenging the rock star lifestyle can be.

chapter 9

BORN FOR THIS

The rise of Paramore wasn't just hard on the band. Right from the start they had constantly stressed how much they valued their fans and strove to have a personal relationship with as many of them as possible. Throughout their career, meet-and-greets had been a regular occurrence, and journalists don't have to look far on the net to find hundreds of personal accounts of meetings with the band, photos, and testaments to their good nature. It's something Paramore take very seriously indeed, as Ashley Brown, founder of the leading Paramore fansite *paramorefans.com* explained to the author. "They just realise how important it is, I think. Everyone wants their band to talk to them and care about them. They're good at fulfilling that."

Paramore's fanbase has generally reciprocated in kind, taking them just as seriously. One user on Twitter even tweeted to note the celebrations of her one-year anniversary of meeting Hayley. But of course, having a personal relationship with every fan that wants one is simply impossible, and would leave the band no time to actually write and play music, let alone take part in the endless stream of promotion that goes hand in hand with success. For Paramore, a crucial way of managing this dichotomy has been the internet. Of course, sites like Myspace have had a huge influence on the way music is accessed and distributed; as Jeremy said in an interview, "Even if you're just a local band, you can get so much recognition. It's just a case of giving someone a link, and they can hear you straight away, whereas if it wasn't [online] you'd have to go through inviting people out and hoping they'd show up. It's helped so much, MySpace is ridiculous, everyone has one, parents have one! It's really cool that it's turned out to be such a big thing." Paramore have used this to its fullest potential, tapping into the social networking and blogging revolutions as a means of demonstrating the respect they have for their fans. It also has a practical function for Hayley: it

allows her to maintain some control of what is said about her in the press. In an interview with *Kerrang!* in 2009, she said: "I'm passionate about writing and I enjoy blogging... I've found that the more connected you are, the more people know you and can call bull when they see it."

But to properly understand the way in which Paramore have used the internet, you must first understand the new environment it has created for music to exist in. Joe Shooman is a music journalist and the author of *Whose Space Is It Anyway?*, a book on social networking sites and their impact on popular culture, particularly music. He explained the huge impact that these sites have had on the music industry: "Social networking sites have fundamentally altered the mix of publicity routes available to any band. The net was always a rather undervalued aspect of the music industry, more than likely because most large labels didn't understand it and were a bit scared of it." He cites the Napster cases of the late 1990s and early 2000s, where the popular file-sharing service was sued and ultimately shut down, as a prime example of major labels' suspicion towards the internet. "Rather than grasping the nettle and making music and acts available to the fans," he explained, "they looked to sue their customers, which is an odd strategy no matter how you look at it."

But it was this set of conditions that allowed for the meteoric rise of MySpace. "MySpace's rise in 2005/6 made it an essential part of any band's activity," continues Shooman, "because for the first time on one page you could have music, videos, gig dates and biographical information, plus an easy URL to navigate to. It changed the net from a blind grope in a darkened city trying to find a certain band's house on a street you might not know the name of, to a well laid-out and brightly lit system, where as long as you knew *myspace.com* and the name of the band you could find them." But this is not the only reason that MySpace thrived, as Joe elaborated. "So far, not so social; the uptake of Myspace was largely down to its interactivity. Bands could blog from the road and fans could comment; bands could comment on comments; fans could email the band members. And because most of the early uptakers of MySpace were indie labels or the groups themselves, this relaxed and informal exchange between band and fan made a direct connection that did not depend on PR machinery or any kind of record label middleman. This had not happened on such a huge level online before and harked back to the days of punk."

Of course, where the fans lead the labels will generally follow, particularly if there's a chance to increase sales. "Seeing this, bigger labels jumped on the bandwagon and every group now has a rather quaint and dated MySpace," Shooman notes. "But also as technology and online networks spring up day by day, then groups, labels and PR took charge and now Facebook, Twitter, Bebo *et al* are essential places for a band to be available. Someone's worked out that fanbases like to be online and like to check out music online… ten years late, but welcome to the party chaps."

Despite their increasing popularity, Paramore have maintained the "relaxed and informal exchange" between band and fan that Joe Shooman describes. Paramore's LiveJournal is incredibly popular, with an active, thriving community of users supporting it. They regularly post comments on Hayley or the band's blogs discussing what was said with one another, or answering questions posed to them. Hayley will sometimes respond to things she has read, too, either addressing users in person, or mentioning their stories as inspirational to her. Ashley Brown, who runs *paramorefans.com*, explained the popularity of the LiveJournal to the author. "It started in the beginning as a really informal way for them to blog and stuff," she said. "It's basically just Hayley's thing. But I think the kids really like it because she just talks like she's just talking to you instead of a formal release thing. When people would comment she would comment back." As Ashley says, it's not just a public diary of the band's movements, though it does serve that purpose. Hayley is acutely aware of her readership, from recommending bands and films, responding to topics of discussion in the forum and even – on one occasion – chastising a user who had photoshopped a picture of her face onto a penis ("Congratulations, sir, you are the world's biggest ass"). As she said in one post: "I am so excited to see that this is actually a community. Not just a forum. The whole point of this thing is to keep it feeling all family-like. That's why it's called an LJ community." The LiveJournal has been an outlet for Hayley during some of her most difficult times: in 2008, she responded to an auction for a handwritten book on eBay that claimed to be hers, written when she was a child. She confirmed that the book was in fact hers, and that the seller was her ex-stepfather. And while she claims that a part of her laughed at the bit of her past that had surfaced, she also admits that she "felt like throwin' shit".

The band's own website functions in a similar way to the LiveJournal. It is not just a place to receive updates and information about the band, it allows for users to become part of a community, where they can upload a profile, share photos and videos with other users, and even arrange meet-ups on the day of shows with people in their area. The band also have their own profiles on the site. It is currently the most trafficked website across all of the Warner Music Group's acts, of which there are over four hundred. Fans are encouraged to visit the website for a whole host of exclusive content and media (*www.paramore.net*).

However, after Paramore's profile increased, a small number of vocal fans began complaining about what they perceived as the changing attitude of the band. It's hard to say if this constitutes a backlash – there's no way of judging how widespread the feelings expressed by these users were – but it is significant in that the LiveJournal community was one of the sites of unrest. A long running discussion broke out at the end of July 2007, when one community member wrote: "I miss the old Paramore SOOO BAD!!!", complaining that they hardly updated their LiveJournal anymore, and had heard numerous reports that Hayley had been "running away" from fans rather than stopping to talk like the "old Hayley" would have. This sparked a wide range of responses from members of the community. They tend to fall somewhere between sympathetic, with users stating that the band have earned their success, have a very high number of commitments and frequently express gratitude for their fans and so on, to more caustic, with members complaining that the band have changed their attitude. Of course, it's not an uncommon trend for a core fanbase to follow a band and then become disgruntled when they achieve mainstream success. One user writes that "to think that when I go back to school everyone will pretty much have mb ['Misery Business'] on their iPods is kind of scary." Fans who were part of the first generation, so to speak, who helped the band establish themselves before they found mainstream popularity, can often feel a sense of entitlement. They can also feel like the band they had invested so much of themselves in is devalued once it is no longer a 'secret' for those 'in-the-know' – even though widespread success should surely confirm, rather than undermine, their initial love of that band. But while these feelings are perfectly common, in Paramore's case, the community had access to a means of discussing them; not just in public, but also in a large arena where it could be potentially damaging to the band.

Paramore's response to this is really a testament to how seriously they take their fanbase. As moderators of the community, they could have deleted the threads so that no one could see them, shut down the community, or simply have ignored them and waited for the discussion to pass. But instead Hayley actually posted a link to the thread on the band's LiveJournal, highlighting the discussion to lots of casual viewers who would not have found it otherwise, and even addressed the issues directly. She stated that the band's relationship with its fans was something they all took very seriously. The notoriously demanding Warped Tour meant they had never been busier in all their lives. She reassured fans that if they couldn't stop to say hello, it wasn't because "we think that playing Wii on our bus would be more worthwhile" but because they are probably on their way to a prior commitment. She finishes by apologising for any upset that people might be feeling, and states that the fans remain the reason they do the band at all. Ashley Brown, founder of *paramorefans.com*, is more dismissive of any upset there might have been in the fanbase. "People talk about that [how the band have changed] a lot," she told me. "I guess when people grow up they change naturally. I guess there'll always be people who don't like the new stuff or don't agree with every little thing that happens."

On the whole Paramore's fanbase remain one of the most devoted and passionate of any contemporary band, and the popularity of long-running fan sites like *paramorefans.com* and *paramore.org* are a testament to this. For example, *paramorefans.com* has around 8,000 members, with a few hundred people who are active on the forums every day. Just like the Paramore LiveJournal, it works like a community, as Ashley explains: "They've all made friends with each other and there are little cliques and stuff. I don't even know a lot of the stuff that goes on there. The fans are dedicated, they love the band. They're like, obsessed with the band." But the reason why they have earned this exceptionally loyal fanbase is perhaps difficult to pin down. "I don't really know," said Ashley when asked. "They're very likeable, if you go to show you have a great time, you fall in love, they're super nice people. They just like, have a little spark about them, they become your favourite band."

But the internet is also home to a few oddities, demonstrating just how far some people's obsession with the band goes. Witness the LiveJournal community 'Paramore Secrets', for example, where users are encouraged to anonymously post their feelings about Paramore, which range from declarations of love to indignant rants and even a spot of Freud-baiting psychobabble. But Ashley diffuses some of the alarm a casual viewer might feel stumbling across this part of the community. "On LiveJournal there are a lot of like 'secret' communities, where you can anonymously submit so they're not afraid to say anything. It's mostly a joke, y'know? It was started as a joke and then some people take it kind of far. It was a funny, inside joke kind of thing, if you weren't a super Paramore fan you wouldn't know the references, kind of thing. But some are creepy, I agree."

If a minority of fans were still sore about the increasing popularity of the band, it wasn't about to get any better for them: Paramore's star was in the ascendancy, and they were facing one their most comprehensive and gruelling tour schedules to date. The Warped Tour stint was completed in mid-August, but the band had little time to rest. That month Hayley, Josh and Jeremy showed some love for new partners in crime New Found Glory by appearing in their video for 'Kiss Me'. A cover of a song American pop-rockers Sixpence None The Richer, the video features a likely lad tallying the kisses he gets from various young women. He even makes a move on Hayley, who sees the tally on his arm and gives him a slap on the face for his trouble. Hayley remembers Warped 2007 as the best summer the band had ever had, and that the last date in Portland had been a depressing farewell. It probably wasn't helped by the slight trepidation the band were feeling about their arrival in England: prior to the tour they would be playing the Reading and Leeds Festivals (which they'd had to cancel the previous year due to Hayley's losing her voice). The Reading festival is the oldest major festival still in existence and now welcomes around 150,000 punk, rock indie and metal fans over two sites on the (usually rain-soaked) August Bank Holiday weekend. But the two dates are as notorious as they are legendary, mainly due to the unofficial tradition of 'bottling' unpopular bands until they are forced offstage (the missiles are often filled with urine). Alumni of this most unwelcome trial include New Jersey kitsch poppers Daphne And Celeste, 50 Cent and Paramore's label mates Panic! At The Disco, though it must be noted that P!ATD did complete their set, despite singer Brendan Urie taking a bottle in the face. Paramore were vocal about their fears they would receive the same treatment, particularly in light of their previous cancellation. But Hayley remained admirably stoic about what was ahead, saying: "We're going to get bottled. That's going to suck, but I won't leave. I swear... I don't care if I'm dying – I will lay down and finish the set." Fortunately, they needn't have worried so much. The band drew a good crowd to the main stage, despite their relatively early slot, and not a bottle was seen to darken the sky.

The band went on to play dates across the UK, including stop-offs in Germany and the Netherlands amongst others. And while the reception of *Riot!* had been lukewarm in the press, since then – due to the amount of fan hysteria and shows selling out – they had begun to take notice of Paramore. A reviewer for *The Big Cheese* at the Manchester show on September 3 reported how tickets for the gig were sold out half an hour after going on sale, and were now being sold for four times their face value. She said that "Hayley has a fantastic voice, which holds up for the entire fifty minutes," and awarded the gig four out of five. *NME* called their live show "utterly brilliant, irresistible and ever so slightly shameful," and *Record Collector* stated, "despite much hype... like their fans, the band are just having fun."

Perhaps the most surprising review came from *Kerrang!*, who in the past had been decidedly frosty in their response. At the end of the year they included Paramore's set at the London Astoria on May 30 (before the release of *Riot!*), in their Top 100 gigs of the previous twelve months. "As tickets changed hands for over £100 outside," they wrote, "500 die hard fans were going mental to one of the most frantic pop-punk shows the venue had seen in years." As if astonished by the admission, the reviewer ends: "No, *really*."

While Paramore were on tour in Europe, they also released the second single from *Riot!*: 'Hallelujah'. The promo was shot by Big TV!, also known as film makers Andy Delaney and Monty Whitbloom, who had previously made videos for Natalie Imbruglia, Dido and Duran Duran. It is a montage of live clips and backstage footage, similar to the video for 'All We Know', and serves as a perfect taste of the band's live show for new fans who hadn't had a chance to see them live. The single was released on September 18 in America, a couple of weeks earlier in the UK, and featured the B-side 'Decoy'. Opening with a lively and infectious riff, before rolling into a lulling verse, the song is a truly excellent example of Paramore's talents – indeed, it's a wonder 'Decoy' wasn't chosen to be released with *Riot!*, though it would become a live favourite with band and fans alike. Despite its relatively upbeat sound, the lyrics concern using a lover who you don't really care for. "It's about how you get into a relationship with someone and maybe you know your heart's not in it, but you see them pouring out every bit of themselves, working really hard to try and make it happen," Hayley admitted. "It shows a bad side of me." The single didn't attract quite as much attention as 'Misery Business', though it managed to maintain the momentum that its predecessor had created.

The rest of the year was filled up with touring and promotion for their new album. The band would travel from Europe to Japan to Australia and then back to the States for another headline tour, a blur of constant travelling, performing and promotion. By the end of the year Paramore had played well in excess of 100 shows. In October, the third single from *Riot!*, 'crushcrushcrush', was premiered on MTV's show *TRL*. The promo was once again shot by Shane Drake and features the band playing in a barren landscape while they are looked upon by anonymous voyeurs. It's all very *The Hills Have Eyes*, the muted colours and desolation of the scene adding menace to an otherwise quite playful song. As it reaches its climax the three

characters watching the band hijack their equipment and triumphantly smash it up, a rock 'n' roll indulgence that Paramore themselves have never really gone for. The single once again did well for the band, reaching Number 4 on the US *Billboard* Hot Modern Rock tracks chart, and ultimately being certified gold in the US in September 2007.

That same month, LA-based alternative rock band Say Anything also released the 27-track *In Defense Of The Genre*, which guest featured a whole host of artists: Gerard Way of My Chemical Romance, Adam Lazzara of Taking Back Sunday, Jordan Pundik and Chad Gilbert from New Found Glory, and one Hayley Williams. It wasn't the first time Hayley had provided guest vocals for a track: in April she had appeared on The Chariot's song 'Then Came To Kill', from the album *The Fiancée*. It is a brutal, complex prog-metal affair, as far from Paramore as you could hope to get while still holding a guitar, and Hayley's haunting drone is hard to compare to her recordings with her own band. Fortunately her appearances on *In Defense Of The Genre* are probably a little more accessible to the average Paramore fan. 'The Church Channel' masquerades as a chirpy pop-punk tune, but structurally (if not melodically) it's surprisingly adventurous. 'Plea' is a quieter affair, the forlorn opening giving way to a big rock chorus. Kenny Vasoli of The Starting Line also provides guest vocals for the song, but both tracks are similar in that Hayley's section is their standout moment.

Another big stand-out moment for the band came in October, when they got the chance to appear on *Late Night With Conan O'Brien* – a hugely popular late night American talk show, which showcases the best and brightest in new alternative music. It was a particular highlight for Hayley, who confesses that Conan is her "celebrity crush," and that she would keep her mother awake late at night as a teen, laughing out loud at the show. Like many great opportunities in music, it came about largely by chance, whilst the band were on the Warped Tour. At the New Jersey date, after completing their set, the band came off stage to find themselves face-to-face with Max Weinberg, known to many Americans as the bandleader and drummer for the Max Weinberg 7, Conan's house band on the show. But he is best known to the world as the drummer of the E Street Band, Bruce Springsteen's outfit, whom Max has accompanied on over ten albums and countless world tours. Max's son, Jay Weinberg, was on the Warped Tour playing drums in a band called The Reveling, and his father had come to the New Jersey date to see

From school friends to arena-fillers.

his son play. They had both stumbled across Paramore's set and Max stuck around afterwards to meet the band. He had particularly fond words to say to Zac, whom he congratulated on the quality of his drumming. It was, in Hayley's words, "so rewarding coming from such an accomplished dude."

Later, Max found the band's bus and mentioned that he'd like to put in a word with Conan's booking agent, to try and get Paramore to play on the show. Hayley revealed on LiveJournal that the opportunity was so exciting it made her want to urinate almost instantly. Nerves can do strange things. Sure enough, some months later the call came that the band had been given the gig, and in October they performed 'Misery Business' to an audience of several million viewers. The band's excitement about the appearance is almost evident in their performance, as Hayley throws herself about the small stage while the band play with their characteristic enthusiasm and passion. It was a moment Hayley confessed to having dreamt about since the band started.

But in Paramore's turbulent career, for every up there seemed to be a down, and one came for Jeremy in December at a show in the UK. His monumental headbanging is one of the most recognisable aspects of the Paramore show – it's more like bodybanging – but it worked against him when, mid-bang, he hit his face against Zac's bass drum mic. He had to finish the set with his lip gushing blood, which later required three stitches. He had some consolation from the nurse, however, who told him there were 25 other kids in A&E that night from the gig, with Paramore-related injuries.

As the year drew to a close, the band were exhausted from the near-constant touring that 2007 had demanded of them. But it had not been without its highlights, of course: *Riot!* had been certified gold, *Alternative Press* had voted 'Misery Business' the best video of 2007, and Hayley had come second to Amy Lee in the *Kerrang!* Reader's Poll for 'Sexiest Female'. But the real high point of the year for the band was to come in December, when Hayley received a phone call from John Janick, head of Fueled By Ramen. Paramore had been nominated for a Grammy in the category of 'Best New Artist'.

The Grammy awards were established in 1958, and have since risen to prominence as the most desirable and esteemed award in America. There are four basic categories: 'Album of the Year,', 'Record of the Year', 'Song of the Year' and 'Best New Artist', though the total number of awards is much higher. Paramore were naturally delighted to receive the nomination; Hayley recalls herself and her flatmate "screaming our heads off" upon hearing the news, and she immediately posted on the band's LiveJournal.

The ceremony was held the following year in February. Paramore lost out to Amy Winehouse, who had a tremendously successful year in 2007, combining millions of sales with general critical acclaim. Winehouse also won 'Record of the Year' and 'Song of the Year', but the band weren't too perturbed about her hogging all the best awards. Hayley stated that although the band didn't get to take home a Grammy, the mere experience of being there was something they could never have hoped to happen so early in the band's life. Besides, they would win two *Teen Choice* Awards in August that year: one for 'Best Rock Track' with 'crushcrushcrush', and one for 'Best Rock Group'. Who needs a Grammy when you can have a *Teen Choice* Award?

Nevertheless, in many ways 2007 had been Paramore's year. They started it holed up in House of Loud with David Bendeth, excitedly laying down the record that would truly put them on the map. By the time it was over, they had headlined the Warped Tour, played Reading and Leeds, completed a world tour taking in Australia and Japan, had three successful singles and a gold album, and received a Grammy nomination. While the band had worked hard to earn their success, building their fanbase from the ground up since they first starting touring in 2005, the release of *Riot!* had catapulted them to international success with astonishing speed.

But despite all the success – or rather, in part because of it – the band were exhausted. As early as the summer, there were signs of the band's weariness, and their schedule had only grown more hectic since then. Josh revealed that at the end of 2007 they badly needed to take a break: "We told everyone that we ain't doing shit once got we home from our headline US tour," he said. "We needed time to relax and be with our families." But the phone kept ringing and Paramore never really got that break – they even spent the end of December playing the MTV New Year Show. The fresh year is supposed to represent new hopes, new challenges, the promise of change. But for Paramore it would only bring the same exhausting promotion for *Riot!* that defined 2007, and it would drive them to the very edge of implosion.

chapter 10

THE LAST PLANE HOME

The year 2008 kicked off with a bang with the UK 'Riot! Tour', which began at the end of January in Manchester. Supporting the band was one of the strongest line-ups Paramore had taken on the road to date. The shows opened with Conditions, a fast and furious melodic punk band from Richmond. Next up was Kids In Glass Houses, a Cardiff-based five-piece that had been making waves and getting considerable coverage in 2007 despite not actually being signed yet. Playing directly before Paramore on most dates (with the odd exception) were their new best buddies, New Found Glory. There had been some upset from die-hard NFG fans that they were playing first – mainly on the grounds that they had been one of the innovators of the pop-punk genre, and had over a decade of experience behind them. But in her typical forthcoming fashion, Hayley was quick to address these concerns, saying: "I think when they realise the friendship we have with them and that we are doing this for the love of music, they'll realise it doesn't matter who is bigger or who did what." New Found Glory were full of praise for Paramore, too, in an interview *The Big Cheese*. Singer Jordan Pundik spoke about how he was instantly a fan on hearing the first record, saying: "They're great songwriters, and catchy as hell… I think that Paramore have staying power for sure."

In a LiveJournal entry Hayley spoke about how the tour was "a total paradise," but in reality there was trouble ahead for them. Elsewhere in the same entry she talked of sides to herself and also "of the dudes" that no one sees, a remark that was not expanded upon but seemed to have some ominous portent for the band. Then came a big shock – on February 21, a LiveJournal entry signed by all five members announced that the remainder of the tour – six dates in all – would be cancelled. The reason was "internal issues that have been going on in this band for quite a while now," which supposedly began when the band were preparing for the US 'Riot! Tour' in October of the previous year. The announcement was vague, saying only that the band felt the cancellation of the tour absolutely necessary to the survival of the group, and that they would keep the fans updated. But news outlets and forums were almost immediately awash with rumours that the band was over – not least MTV, who on the same day posted an article on their website with the opening line, "Are Paramore calling it quits?"

It was a tense time for Paramore fans, until on February 22 another message was posted on the band's LiveJournal. "We weren't saying the band was over," it emphatically stated, instead saying they felt honesty was the best policy with fans. They insisted that they would be hitting the road again in March to fulfil their touring commitments, and that the time off was being well used to get the band on the right track. There was no clarification or further explanation, and it would be months later when fans actually started to hear the full story. On February 26, Zac was posting about his excitement for the upcoming tour, saying that while he appreciated all the phone calls and encouragement from friends and fans alike, he was now looking to move on. The message was clear: things had been bad in the Paramore camp, but they were going to keep plodding on – and they certainly weren't about to elaborate on what had actually happened.

Later Hayley would speak of the furore the announcement had made: "We tried to be as honest as we could with it, without giving our life stories," she said, "and it definitely did come back to bite us. But in the end, it was the best thing for us to do, to communicate with our fans that we needed time… We didn't like cancelling shows, but that's what it took; to go home and kind of start over again."

She revealed that the first announcement was written at the airport in Paris waiting to board a plane home, while the band were not only dealing with their "internal issues," but also the frustration at having to let a lot of people down. Their mood had definitely filtered through into the web entry. Taylor even revealed that in the back of his mind he was wondering if this was the last plane home he would be boarding from a Paramore tour.

"It was really tough, and we wanted to nip it in the bud before it got too bad," Josh told *Ultimate Guitar* in 2009. We were like, 'Let's just go home and fix these problems before they get worse.' Most bands kind of ignore it, try to go on, and pretend like it's not even there. We were

like, 'Dude, we don't want to be those bands.'"

In addition to the strains of the schedule, a further reason for the trouble at this time has only come to light recently. Throughout Paramore's career they have been honest and up front about a variety of issues, but they have also zealously guarded certain aspects of their private lives. While Hayley's childhood has been fairly well documented in the press, the background of the other band members are not generally discussed. And one area that is very rarely touched upon is the band's relationships. You don't have to look hard to find a whole host of unfounded rumours on the internet detailing the status of Josh and Hayley's relationship. Some insist that they are simply very close friends, not least because they write their songs together.

Speaking about the gossip that they were in fact dating, Josh told *Alternative Press* in 2008: "People are obsessed with that, but we're not. Everyone in the band all had crushes on her when they were in high school, but she's not that type of girl. There are really so many attractive things about her; she's fun to be around, has a good personality and of course, she's cute, so I can see why people think that." But despite their insistence to the contrary, the speculation was persistent. The internet was awash with fan stories about a romantic tryst between the pair, suggesting it was more an expression of what people want to believe rather than what is actually the case. Either way, the band were keeping tight-lipped about it.

That is until October 2009. Paramore did a cover shoot for *Alternative Press* following the late September release of their third album and in the article, Josh and Hayley finally admitted to having had a relationship – an almost three year one, in fact, which finally ended in late 2007. Ashley Brown, who founded and runs *paramorefans.com*, explained that this was in fact widely known amongst long-running fans of the band. "Oh yeah, like, everyone knew. People who had liked them forever knew. And then it was like, oh my gosh, I hope they don't break up and the band quits, y'know? You could tell that something happened, but they never talked about it." Paramore maintain that the fallout of the break up wasn't the only reason for the cancellation of the tour, but concede it was a part of it. In a disarmingly honest interview, they also revealed that they kept the relationship a secret initially because they feared it would be seen as a "big joke" by the outside world. "We didn't want the band to be about me and Hayley being in a relationship together," Josh said, "because then the band would be about our relationship, not our music. It distracts people from the whole point of being in a band."

They don't detail exactly why the relationship broke down – Josh speaks of how he feels that he has been "forced into the world" of fame, that his personal life is sacred to him, and that no one has any claim to details of his life. What is known is that Hayley is now openly dating Chad Gilbert, guitar player and songwriter for New Found Glory.

The break-up was difficult on everyone involved, but they now maintain that it was the only way for them to progress. "It was either going to be the Josh and Hayley extravaganza and turn into a soap opera or it was going to turn into a full fledged band with each of us being our own puzzle piece,"

Hayley and Chad.

Hayley said. "It works better this way. It's way healthier."

Once they arrived home, they took some time apart to gain a little perspective. The band even began seeing a counsellor, who imparted to them the importance of communicating with one another. There was so much that the individual members felt they had to say to one another that the counsellor barely had to speak: "All he had to do was ask one question and then he wouldn't even talk the rest of the time!" Zac revealed. After these emergency measures, Paramore finally reached a place where they were ready to continue. They weren't exactly back to full strength – any bad feelings that lingered following this episode would later resurface and threaten the band's future once again. But for the time being, Paramore were fighting fit once again.

The fourth single to be released from *Riot!* would be 'That's What You Get', the rousing anthem and one of the album's highlights. The band shot a promo with Marcos Siega in Nashville, Tennesee at a house belonging to their friends The Paper Route. The video shows the band at their most comfortable: the theatrical stage demeanour you see in the 'Misery Business' or 'crushcrushcrush' videos is toned down, the band performance looks more like a rehearsal than a show. Paramore surrounded themselves with friends and family for the shoot, a move which was no doubt helpful given the somewhat fragile state of the band; as Hayley said, it felt more like a "hangout session." All of this, added to the domestic setting, makes 'That's What You Get' feel the most personal of all their videos, a sense that Hayley got too. "I think this is the first time you're gonna get to see who we really are," she told *MTV News*. The single was released to radio on March 24, peaking at Number 66 on the *Billboard* Hot 100 and 36 on the *Billboard* Hot Modern Rock Tracks. It once again did well on a number of platforms, particularly channels like Fuse TV and the college station MTVu in the States and *Kerrang!* TV in the UK.

The next big tour was with Jimmy Eat World. As a long-standing fan, Hayley had spoke in the past about her ambitions to tour with the band, only half in jest. She had first met them in December 2007 after a show, and had ultimately ended up singing on stage with them the night after. Paramore had also covered the band's single 'Sweetness' on the 'Riot! Tour'. But what started as a pipedream had quickly become a reality, and the band would soon be co-headlining with one of the group's that they claim made Paramore possible. The magnitude of the achievement was also a boost for the band after their recent tribulations: "What better way to come back from all this?" Josh told *MTV News*. The first date was on April 1 and the tour continued throughout that month and into the start of May. Also on the road was Dear And The Headlights, Jimmy Eat World's fellow Arizonians, and it seemed to have some sort of therapeutic effect on the band: Hayley stated that it had been one of the most enjoyable and relaxing tours they'd been on. Following the completion of the tour, Paramore returned to Europe for some more festival dates. The first booking was to headline the 'Give It A Name Festival', the very same one that they had appeared at much lower down the bill in 2006. It was a huge deal for the band, as it had hosted their first trip to the UK; it must have felt like a homecoming of sorts. This time it was to be held in London, as before, but also in Sheffield. The bill featured 30 Seconds To Mars, Plain White T's, Long Islander hardcore outfit Glassjaw and cult punkers Alkaline Trio, amongst a whole host of others. Following this Paramore headed to Dublin for a show to 6,000 fans, their first ever show in Ireland, where they were also presented with gold plaques for their Ireland sales of *Riot!*. They also played shows at Radio 1's One Big Weekend and Rock am Ring in Germany, before heading out to get a small dose of The Warped Tour – only six dates this time, but Hayley couldn't quite get through the year without a taste of her favourite festival.

Starting on July 28, the band embarked 'The Final Riot! Tour', the last stint they would do in promotion of their second album. It had been a difficult year for the band so far, with touring being near continuous and time to themselves in short supply. As Hayley told *Rock Sound* in March, "Right now the biggest challenge is fighting for time off… we started taking it in turns to go crazy but that eventually got us fighting a lot. We know we need to be thankful for what we have, we are. But it is hard to figure out the line of being grateful for it and knowing that if you take everything you are offered you will not last doing it." But all the same, they felt like they had one final trek around the States in them for a fanbase that had increased exponentially in size even since the relase of *Riot!*. Their workload might have taken its toll on the band, but it had certainly had the desired effect in terms of the ever-increasing popularity of the band. There would be 21 dates over 19 states, and it would turn out to be the last chance to see Paramore in their current incarnation.

Travelling with Paramore were three support acts: Paper Route (who had provided the house for the 'That's What You Get Video'), Phantom Planet (who had shot to fame with the song 'California', which provided the theme tune for the immensely popular teen drama *The OC*) and Jack's Mannequin, originally the side project of Something Corporate vocalist Andrew McMahon (but one which had quickly gained a strong following of its own with some breezy piano-led pop rock). On this tour Paramore decided it was finally time to fulfil their ambition of producing a live DVD, and this they did during their Chicago show at the Congress Theatre on August 12. The DVD was simply entitled *The Final Riot!* and gives a fascinating insight into life on the road with the band, as well as showing how far their presence as a live act had developed since first appearing, fresh faced and eager, in 2005.

If fans with tickets to 'The Final Riot! Tour' were concerned they might

see a band worn down and indifferent, these doubts were most likely blown away as soon as the opening song. *The Final Riot!* shows a band utterly at the height of their powers – confident, water-tight, magnetic and explosive. It's hard to know how the far the well-documented troubles in the band were affecting its members at this time, but if they were, the DVD also shows a group of consummate professionals who are completely committed to putting on a great performance. Hayley is of course the centre point of the whole show, as any front person has to be in a live act. But the intro sends out a clear message. Josh begins by repeating a simple guitar riff, the theatre dark but for three spotlights illuminating him. Taylor then comes in to accompany him on the opposite side of the stage, lit in the same way, before Jeremy and Zac explode into a salvo of furious rhythms. In front of the audience's eyes, the Paramore sound is being constructed piece by piece. By the time Hayley bounds on stage to a roar from the crowd that must have shook the foundations of the venue, everyone is thinking the same thing: Paramore is band, just like the T-shirts in 2005 insisted, and each member is as vital as the last.

Opening with 'Born For This' says something too – it says 'This is for you, we're on this stage because of our fans and for the pleasure of our fans'. They tear through the song with an urgency that proves they mean it, before launching into 'That's What You Get'. By this time the crowd is a single entity, bouncing up and down in unison like some bizarre ritual of worship for the band. Hayley stalks the stage throughout with an assurance that overwhelms her diminutive frame and makes her seem ten feet tall. Never standing still, she is the pied piper leading the crowd, jumping up and down with them one minute, thrusting out the mic to insist they sing the next. But for all her effervescent energy – throwing her fiery hair about in arcs of orange, punching the air, skipping from one side of the stage to other – she retains an air of real femininity. She might head bang with the best of them, but she also struts, sways and jives with an allure that you rarely see at a rock show.

Her voice is a marvel, too. She can hit every note heard on record with the same power live, which is all the more amazing given the way she throws herself around. Her voice is rawer and throatier on stage, which lends itself well to the forcefulness of the live sound. But she's not the only one that impresses wth her professionalism: Paramore sound like a band that have been touring well beyond their three or four years. Josh and Taylor's guitar sound is even more muscular and crisp than it is on record, the melodies shining through when they need to and the riffs slamming down when they must. Jeremy draws the eye: after Hayley he's the most natural performer, regularly marching right up to the edge of the stage to keep the energy levels of the fans up. At the back of the stage Zac is elevated and always well-lit, and with his emphatic, aggressive drum style, he looks and sounds like the engine of the band. On stage it is Zac who is responsible for the pace and energy of the songs, and he plays solidly for around an hour with the same power; his stamina is incredible.

In between songs Hayley has the charisma and spirit of an evangelist preacher, rousing the crowd as she instructs them to raise their hands, or scream, or sing along with her. This is the main difference from the early Paramore: her crowd control, the confidence to stand in front of thousands of people and know that she can keep every one's attention. An early *NME* review called a gig "merchandised power-pop that's one big red foam hand short of the stadiums in Hayley's head," which is a cutting way of noting the slick theatrics of the performance. Paramore weren't an up-and-coming band anymore though, throwing themselves around the ShiraGirl Stage at Warped Tour or the Birmingham Academy 2 in a bid to win their fans one by one. They had become an international rock band, and they weren't shy of giving their fans a show. From the giant RIOT! lights suspended above the stage to the ramp that runs behind it, from where Hayley sings 'Let the Flames Begin', every flash of light, note played and line sung has been rehearsed to make an impact. This couldn't be more evident on the more reflective moments of the show, like the acoustic version of 'My Heart', where shafts of light dramatically illuminate Hayley, eyes closed, fists clenched. She directs the audience in a chorus of "whoahs", encouraging them to sing louder until you can't hear Josh's guitar anymore. Likewise for the cover of Leonard Cohen's 'Hallelujah': this isn't a sweaty little punk show. This is stadium rock territory. Regardless, the closing moments of 'Misery Business' send the crowd into a frenzy, and as the band join hands and take a bow, you have to admit that they've mastered playing to huge crowds just like they mastered playing to small ones.

Yet what makes *The Final Riot!* so good as a DVD is the insight it gives into the touring life beyond what happens on stage. The band reveals the process of preparing for what was one of the most difficult tours they had ever put together. The pressure of knowing it would be last tour from *Riot!* was getting to the band, and we see the difficulty they have in preparing an intro. Josh says that he considers the intro one of the most important elements of the show; after a couple of false starts the band comes up with one they like, until Hayley shows up and says she doesn't like it. We see the band get frustrated and squabble, and it's a fascinating look at how difficult even the smallest, seemingly insignificant aspect of the band's lives can be. We also get a look at life on the bus, and the way that Hayley copes with being the only girl in a crew of over a dozen. Although she reveals that she has never toured with another girl on the bus and that there are times when she feels like ripping her hair out, she equitably states that she thinks the guys have it worst. But despite the male members of the band being tantalisingly close to "dude freedom," Josh states that for the most part, Hayley is just another one of the guys. And you really get to see the part of life in a band that everyone envies: not having to grow up, just like Zac observes, as the five members trek from city to city, mucking about and generally looking like they're having the time of their lives. We also see the band get presented with their RIAA platinum plaques in New York in July, to celebrate *Riot!* having sold over one million copies in the United States.

The DVD would not be released until November, a few months after it was filmed, and also came with an audio CD of the concert. Paramore had in fact already released a live album entitled *Live In The UK 2008*, which was recorded and sold during the UK '*Riot!* Tour' with New Found Glory. But that record was limited to a very small number of copies, and there was clearly a demand beyond this exclusive pressing. *The Final Riot!* DVD was ultimately certified gold in March of 2009, signifying over half a million sales in the US.

One might think that after the 2008 Paramore had experienced, they would be ready to head underground and disappear off the radar for a while. But a platinum award for *Riot!*, a stint on the Warped Tour and three headline tours (one of which they didn't manage to complete), wasn't quite enough for the band. Turning themselves into a phenomenon was all well and good, but they still had time to become part of another one.

chapter 11

TWILIGHT HOURS, DARKEST HOURS

A high school cafeteria. A trio of girls sit chatting and giggling at a table. One is new to the school; she is shy and slightly deferential, but comfortable with her outsider status, and very pretty in a plain sort of way. She spots a group of striking looking characters entering the cafeteria and enquires to her friends who they are. There is a touch of high school mythology about them; they are foster children of the mysterious Dr. Cullen, they are all in quasi-incestuous relationships with one another, they are exceptionally pale. Then the final Cullen walks in, who immediately catches our heroine's eye. He swaggers through the room in dark colours, a sly half-smile across his muted lips. He has a jaw and cheekbones that might have been carved out of stone, piercing eyes, and a masculine Roman nose to counterbalance his perfectly quaffed hair. He is aloof and unobtainable, but their eyes meet as he casts her a surly gaze. The camera slowly zooms in. The alt-rock influenced soundtrack swells. Sparks fly.

This is the substance of millions of teenage girl's fantasies across the world, not to mention many older women, and a few gentlemen too. This is a scene from *Twilight*, the multi-multi-*multi*-million grossing adaptation of Stephanie Meyer's bestselling novel, which has become an obsession for a whole legion of indoctrinates the world over. The film became the sleeper hit of the new Millennium when it was released in 2008, taking over $7 million in ticket sales on midnight showings from its opening date alone. Since the release of the book in 2005, interest in the franchise had snowballed to the point where it could legitimately be called a sensation, and despite general critical chagrin, the *Twilight* saga is currently one of the most valuable in the film world.

The plot concerns Bella Swan, a teenage girl who finds the monotony of her life injected with a little vampiric magic when she meets Edward Cullen, a 108-year-old blood sucker who might have a face from classical sculpture, but knows when to get rough, too: specifically, when heroically saving Bella from other, more unpleasant vampires.

While no one quite predicted the runaway success of *Twilight*, it was always billed to be a teen film, and the lead single from the soundtrack was bound to get a lot of attention. Hayley was personally excited about the project; she had loved the books which were the first series she had ever read (she never got into Harry Potter, despite being a fan of the films). Josh had already sent Hayley some music that she thought suited the tone of the books, so in September they decided to head into the studio and record some tracks for a shot at the soundtrack, at the Blackbird Studio in Nashville. Once the song was recorded, they set about trying to get it in the hands of the right people, which didn't happen at first – in fact, they were told to just give up on the idea altogether. But eventually the two songs they submitted – entitled 'Decode' and 'I Caught Myself' – found the right people, were accepted for the soundtrack, and 'Decode' was selected to be the lead single for the film.

In terms of finding inspiration for the songs, Hayley took her cue from the books: "I think I've been a bit like Bella's character before," she said. "A bit melodramatic about certain things and completely careless about other things. Those two extremes are very familiar to me, so pulling from past personal experiences and emotions made it easy to connect with her and say what I needed to say through her." 'Decode' is a big, moody, mid-tempo rock song in the spirit of 'Conspiracy' or 'Let The Flames Begin'. Opening with a sparse and tense guitar riff, the verse is taut and angsty, but with a dream-like quality to it. The chorus is pleading and urgent, the rhythms direct, but the highlight of the song is the all-too-brief breakdown at its close: huge power chords are accented by stomping drum beats, while Hayley's vocal is almost a mesmerising chant. It's one of Paramore's strongest songs to date, and proved that as exhausted as they might have been from the year, they were still brimming with a pressing creativity as songwriters. Eloquent and powerful lyrically, it is perhaps the first indication of where Paramore might be heading next.

'I Caught Myself' has a similar feeling of edginess to 'Decoy', but strives for a more complex, airy sound than the band had previously attempted. It's a deceptively ambitious song that moves though a variety of textures, using repetitive guitar refrains to build up the sound in layers while a skipping drum beat drives the verse forward. The perfectly formed hooks keep the song catchy and accessible while it builds to a huge final thirty seconds, with Hayley sounding defiant above a pounding, simple rock chord progression. It's a great mix of pop sensibility and experimentation that only reveals itself on successive listens, and manages to evoke a wide array of senses: desire, desperation and indignance, beautiful fantasy and cold harsh reality.

Songs inspired by books and for film soundtracks ought not to work: they ought to be stilted and awkward, show the band going through the motions for the sake of a shameless cash-in. But regardless of what you think of *Twilight*, something about the film fired the band's imagination. Particularly on 'I Caught Myself', Paramore push and pull their sound in different directions to startlingly powerful effect. For fans, it was a huge relief – the band might have been going through hard times, but they were writing better music than ever. It's not going too far to say that the strife of the previous months comes through in these two songs; they're forlorn, angry and anguished, musically and lyrically, but they're still held together by Paramore's unfailing sense of melody and structure.

A video for 'Decode' was shot in Nashville, once again with Shane Drake at the helm. The performance segment has the band playing in the clearing of a forest, stalking around through the trees vampire-style, and generally looking meaner and moodier than they ever had before. Cut with clips from the *Twilight* film, it's an atmospheric promo that captures the tone of the song and the movie well, tracking cameras and muted colours creating a suspenseful, restless sensation. The single would be released on November 16 in the US and December 13 in the UK, entering the US *Billboard* Hot Modern Rock tracks chart at Number 35 and peaking at Number 5 – their third Top Twenty single on that chart. It managed to peak at 52 on the UK singles chart, but did best in Finland, where it reached Number 9. In July of 2008 it was certified gold in the US. Perhaps not surprisingly, *Twilight: Original Motion Picture Soundtrack* did exceptionally well, debuting at Number 1 on the *Billboard* 200, and is currently certified platinum twice over. Paramore shared the platform with a varied mix of other artists, from nu-metal superstars Linkin Park to ex-Jane's Addiction singer Perry Farrell and British psychedelic-pop act The Black Ghosts (retailer Hot Topic's release of 'Decode' would also feature the Black Ghost's song 'Full Moon').

It's hard to pinpoint exactly what the associations with *Twilight* did for Paramore. It certainly pleased existing fans, not least because of the quality of the songs they provided; and it definitely exposed them to a new market, though how far this demographic already overlapped with their existing fanbase is unclear. Paramore would be forever bound to *Twilight* in the eyes of many people, and Hayley remarked, "I'm really glad that our band gets to be part of the phenomenon." All the same, with the release of *Twilight*'s sequel *New Moon* pending at the time of writing, Josh explained to *Billboard* magazine why they wouldn't be contributing to the next soundtrack: "We don't want to be, like, the vampire house band."

While *Twilight* was igniting the passions of would-be juvenile vampire lovers the world over, Paramore had taken their first trip to South America for a tour. Beginning on October 17 and stopping off in Chile, Mexico and Brazil, it was an exotic end to their touring commitments for 2008. In November, Hayley and Jeremy attended the Woodie Awards, the annual awards show for the MTVu college television channel. Voted for by fans of

the channel, Paramore won in the most coveted category, 'Woodie of the Year.' They had been nominated alongside all the big names of 2008 – the likes of Lil Wayne, MGMT and Santogold – so winning was a real coup. It had been their only award since the *Teen Choice* Awards earlier in the year, and Hayley was noticeably delighted in her LiveJournal entry that night. She even got the chance to publicly denounce the fashion faux pas of the 'Misery Business' video while presenting the 'Best Video Award'. "Y'know, it's pretty crazy how much of an influence one video can be on so, so many people. I think if we were to realise that, we probably would've chosen to wear something besides those hideous, two sizes too tight, yellow and red jeans. I don't know what we were thinking!"

Paramore were certainly not interested in revisiting the past. Since mid-2008 they had begun sharing ideas for the new record, and while *Riot!* had done exceptionally well for them, it was time to end that chapter of their career. "I'm ready to move on," Hayley told *Alternative Press*. "I think we got everything we could have possibly got from that record."

Aside from the odd show over the Christmas period – one being the Jingle Ball extravaganza at the legendary Madison Square Garden in New York, where the band got to meet Bruce Springsteen – Paramore kept their head down into New Year. In early February 2009, they headed into a studio to begin pre-production on the new record. They had decided it would be recorded in Nashville, the first to be made on home turf. And this time around, they hadn't asked a producer to come and work with them for pre-production, the period where the band write and rehearse in preparation for going into the studio. But a producer had been chosen – Rob Cavallo, who had worked with the band for 'Decode'. A native of Washington D.C., his father had been a successful band manager, so Rob was always likely to go into the industry. At a young age he moved to LA, just in time for the rise of Hair Metal, which was centred around the Sunset Strip in Hollywood – after playing in a few local bands himself, he would begin his career as producer with these bands. As the 1980s died away and took the testosterone-fuelled hi-jinks of Hair Metal with it, Cavallo turned his attention to alternative rock and punk, and it was in these arenas that he would make a name for himself.

He is probably best known as the man behind every Green Day record since *Dookie* in 1994, with the partial exception of *Warning*, for which he was executive producer. The massive success of *Dookie*, Green Day's major label debut, would open Cavallo to a whole host of new opportunities, some credible, some bizarre. Jawbreaker, from San Francisco, had garnered a considerable cult following by 1995, when they headed into the studio with Cavallo to record their major label debut *Dear You*. Despite the acclaim the record attracted, it would be Jawbreaker's last, disbanding after a year of touring the new songs. But the album has gone on to be a kind of musician's favourite, with fans in Fall Out Boy, Brand New, Sparta, Foo Fighters and – of course – Paramore. On the flip side of the coin, Cavallo had done some work on Paris Hilton's excremental *Paris*, an ill-fated attempt to move into music that was heckled by almost every corner of the media. But the crisp, robust sound of 'Decode' had obviously convinced Paramore that Cavallo was their man.

The band went into the studio with Taylor York as a new, full-time member. After Hunter's departure, the band were hesitant about immediately announcing Taylor as an official part of the band, even though

Award ceremony regulars.

he had a writing credit on *Riot!* (for 'That's What you Get'). The last thing they wanted was for fans to get attached to yet another member who may subsequently decide to leave – Taylor may have been an old friend, but he had still missed out on the first three years of the band's career. Yet after two years of touring, he had become just as much a part of Paramore as any other, and they would later announce his official induction into the fold. "We recognize the fact that it's way overdue," the statement would begin. "The four of us (Hayley, Zac, Josh and Jeremy) are proud to announce that Taylor York, a touring member of Paramore for over two years, is now an official member of the band!" Taylor compared the new commitment to entering a relationship. "This might be a terrible analogy," he would later say, "but it's like when you're single and people in relationships say to you, 'Trust me dude, enjoy being single. Enjoy the freedom.'"

If the band was like a relationship, it was a tumultuous one. Writing for the third album was not going well at all. Hayley had imagined that writing for the new record would be a relatively straightforward task – she'd pen a few tunes in her spare time, and before she knew it, they would be written. But despite the hasty patching-up of differences that had occurred after the February 2008 tour cancellation with New Found Glory, relationships in the band were still strained; at the end of touring for *Riot!*, they had reached the point where various members disliked one another, some were not even talking once they left the stage, and all the joys of being in a band had seemingly dissipated. As you might expect, these were not the ideal conditions for creativity. What's more, Hayley was used to working with Josh in extremely close quarters but the process had now completely changed. Hayley and Josh were no longer working like that; she was left to her own devices much of the time, working on songs on her own in her apartment, locking herself away for days on end. It was an experience she found very lonely.

Going into the practice room with the rest of the band didn't make her feel any less lonely, either. There were still some things left to say after the years of close proximity; the air needed to be cleared, there were multiple frustrations that were clogging the channels of creative communication within the band. But Paramore were mentally and physically exhausted from spending the majority of two years on the road together, non-stop. The last thing they felt like doing was sitting down and discussing their problems with one another. So instead, they fought. They tried to plough on in the manner they had before, but the songs simply weren't coming together in the way they felt they should. The pressure that naturally came after the success of *Riot!* wasn't helping either. "Josh and I hadn't written for a while – besides what we did for *Twilight*," Hayley said. "And all of a sudden we were all in a room together, like 'Hey! Let's make a record that's bigger than *Riot!* All these people are expecting it.'" The fact that they were in pre-production without a producer to guide or motivate them was only making things worse, and they took the stress of the whole situation out on one another. "We were all so heated and frustrated with the process," Hayley remembered. Rob Cavallo began making appearances at the studio to try and push the band forward, but they weren't making any headway. Things were looking desperate; Hayley admitted in *Kerrang!* to having doubts at this point that the band would even complete the record.

Circumstances changed when one of Cavallo's studio engineers (the assistants who are crucial in aiding the producer during an album's recording) had some family issues that meant he would not be able to travel down to Franklin to record the album. It was a week before they were due to begin, and the band were forced to make the snap decision to pack up and leave their hometown three days later. They headed to Cavallo's Lightning Sound Studios at his home in Hidden Hills, California. Despite the last minute change of plan, it actually ended up working in the band's favour. "As cool a thing as it was to drive five minutes down the road and work on the record," Hayley said, "it became really... just like... maybe sterile?" Hayley revealed that Emac Studios, where the band had been working, had become "sort of dungeon-like" for the band.

The change of scenery reflected a change in Hayley's attitude to the new record, too. She had been having a real struggle with the lyrics for new songs. In a LiveJournal entry she revealed the insecurities she was battling at the time: "No one wants to hear me whine." During these moments of uncertainty, she found herself visiting chat rooms and talking to long-time fans of the band, sharing little scraps of lyrics she had been working on. The support that they offered gave her the confidence to start saying things that previously she thought she couldn't. She had expressed the same concerns to her mum, who had offered the simple but sage advice, "What you feel can't be wrong." Hayley then began writing more plainly spoken expressions of how she felt than she had ever done before. The problem was, some of it was about her band mates.

"Hayley started bringing in some lyrics that were saying pretty harsh things about us," Josh said. "It was so hard because what she was saying about us was hurtful." But the raw honesty of the lyrics Hayley started sharing was the prompt for the band to begin communicating with one another again. They started talking about how they felt, discussing with one another all of the things they had been through together and how their friendships had been worn away by the stresses of the touring lifestyle; it turned into what Josh describes as a "counselling session." Hayley agrees. "I'm most proud of these lyrics because they were the healer," she told *Kerrang!* in May 2009. She later spoke of these songs and their lyrics as acting as some kind of therapist, forcing the band to talk.

The band began recording in March 2009 and promptly finished in May. After all the long months of frustration and bitterness, of exhaustion and upset, of feeling like what should be the most fun job in the world had become the most difficult, the band had turned a corner. With all of their grievances out in the open, they were ready to get busy making what would turn out to be the most honest, revealing and brilliant album of their career. As Ashley Brown, founder of *paramorefans.com* explains, "It's their whole life, you know. They've been doing it since they were like fifteen, it's all they know and they really, really care about it."

Most importantly, the *spark* that the band had, that they felt in the early days in the Farro's spare room when they first played together, was back. While Josh and Hayley were no longer an item, they still had a connection as songwriters. "The chemistry was always there and always will be," Josh said, a statement which Hayley backed up in the ever-supportive *Alternative Press*: "Josh and I have always been close. My whole musical life I've spent with these guys and with Josh, and we've always had a great relationship. Just because one part of it didn't work out doesn't mean we can't have a great creative relationship, and go on being better off than we ever were… There's not really much that can stand between the way Josh and I write songs together."

chapter 12

SEEING THE WORLD THROUGH BRAND NEW EYES

Brand New Eyes (stylized on the artwork as *brand new eyes*) is a bold title for a bold album. Like a lot of the songs, it is a title that is irrevocably bound to Paramore's experience of making the record. It's not that you need to know about the trials that they endured, the incredibly difficult birth of *brand new eyes*, to enjoy it – but knowing helps you understand how intensely, bravely and beautifully honest it is. It is self-referential, an album about making an album; but it's also an album which is universally meaningful, that takes the raw electricity of a given feeling on a given day and transmits it, powerfully and movingly, to the listener. As Hayley said in *Kerrang!*, "We have never written a record that is so true to exactly where we are right now. I'm excited about people hearing all of these songs because they all tell one big story. They explain everything perfectly." *brand new eyes* is not just Paramore's best album. It is an incredible album, period.

Ironically, the title was born of a song that didn't quite make the cut for the record, its key lyric being, "I lost all my friends since they got brand new eyes." The original reference is perhaps directed at Hayley's band mates – how their possibly changed perspectives might have alienated and isolated her. But the album charts a remarkable transformation, from strife and distress in its early stages to the triumph and joy of coming through dark times toward its close, with every shade and subtlety plotted in between. *brand new eyes* reflects this renewed optimism and hope for the future. Other titles had been considered – one being *Misguided Ghost*, which actually appears as a track on the record, another *The Backwards Race* – but as soon as it was suggested, the band knew that *brand new eyes* would be the title of the record. "It just felt so right, right away," Hayley said.

The album opens with 'Careful', which was the first song the band recorded after entering the studio. You don't have to imagine the release, the explosion of energy that they must have felt laying down the first track for the record after all that they'd been through. You can hear it in 'Careful'. It continues the trend of Paramore opening songs – no intro, no build-up, just straight into a hair-raising rock track, like 'All We Know' and 'For A Pessimist, I'm Pretty Optimistic'. The riff is caustic and dissonant, the rhythms furious, and the track only momentarily stops for breath as Hayley's vocal comes in. It's some vocal, too; one of the most aggressive she has given, she seems to almost spit out the words in the verses. The chorus is pleading and rousing, the brilliant vocal hook dancing around a salvo of machine-gun fire drumming. Every performance in the song is no-holds barred. The dynamics range from loud to really loud, and it rages along at a relentless pace. Cavallo's production leaps out of the speakers at the listener, too: the guitar sound is roaring and full, and the drums are positively thunderous. 'Careful' was in fact one of the first demos Hayley received from Josh for the new record, and she was initially unsure about it. But it quickly came together – the chorus in only five minutes – and it stands as one of the best songs Paramore have written.

'Ignorance' appears next, and is without a doubt the angriest song on the record. There's no introspection or soul-searching; it's full of spite, scorn and fury, but despite this, it is probably the song that saved Paramore. It came about in one practice session, when Hayley remembers Josh was feeling particularly despondent, telling his band mates, "Listen, guys, I'm never gonna to write another song like 'Misery Business', so get over it." But he started playing the opening riff, Hayley took it away, and the rest is history. She describes it as "word-vomit put to guitars and spastic drumming," which is basically as accurate as you can get. 'Ignorance' almost embodies a vehement, purging rant – it moves through a variety of sections, more than can be called verse-chorus, but with a determination and speed that mimics the venting of some serious spleen. The riffs cut and thrust around the direct rhythms while Hayley sings about feeling persecuted and singled out by her band mates. Once again she demonstrates a willingness to thrash her vocal chords a bit. Her voice had always been powerful, but now she was exploring a new range: the register of pissed off.

After two pretty intense songs – first the heaviest, then the angriest that

Paramore have ever written – the album takes a break from beating the listener over the head. The verse of 'Playing God' trips along on a melancholy, picked guitar line, and Hayley's singing sounds forlorn and troubled. But the brilliant chorus combines irresistible pop melodies with some really tough lyrics, Hayley is raging against judgmental people as she threatens to bend or snap off the next finger pointed at her. It's a great juxtaposition, the backing harmonies almost twee against the defiance of the words. This is what Hayley loves most about it. "The song, at its core, is very angry," she explained. "I'm ripping at self-righteous people, ripping at my own band mates and anyone who ever made me feel not good enough. But the overall tone of the song is completely different. It's laid-back and really fun." It was written in Josh and Zac's house, where Taylor and Josh started picking out the guitar part. It reminded the band of Jimmy Eat World, so obviously they all loved it. Hayley had had the lyrics for some time, and while in her head they were for a song that was fast and heavy, something about the music brought them to mind. It is, for Hayley at least, a song that Paramore had wanted to write for a long time.

Future single 'Brick By Boring Brick' initially masquerades as a robust, emotional punk rock tune. The simple power chord intro yields to a great lead guitar melody, while the verse struts on a growling bass line. But the pre-chorus introduces a more evocative, sensitive side to the song, before ushering in the huge chorus. Hayley almost howls as she sounds yearning and despondent, the vocal line athletic and catchy but heart-wrenching, while the textured guitar parts move under her. After the chorus there is a snarling round of 'ba da dahs' that begs to be screamed by a rabid crowd. Lyrically it concerns a girl who isolates herself from reality, protecting herself from harm by building up the walls of a fantasy world. Hayley remembers the first time she heard the song in rehearsal, immediately falling in love with the verses ("it reminded me of mewithoutYou," she explained). She didn't sleep the night after she first heard it, yet had difficulty coming up with a chorus that she felt did justice to the music. The lyrics in the chorus finally came to Hayley when she imagined the girl finally doing away with all of her comforting illusions, "burying everything she'd made up in her mind so she could face the real world for once." Hayley is keen to stress that the song is not autobiographical.

'Turn It Off' is strange one. The main instrumental hook is a jaunty kind of indie-rock riff, similar to 'Here We Go Again' from *All We Know Is Falling*. The verse is electrifying; lyrically elegant, it glides on a marching band-style snare drum beat tailor-fitted to a neat bass line. It is one of Josh's favourite moments on the album, as he explained to *Kerrang!*: "I just love what happens musically and melodically during the verse of this song... Everything together just moves you." But the chorus is where things take a turn for the worse. Despite its dark lyrical content, it has an irritating, yelping quality that undermines its emotional power. It wanders a little too close to pop-rock mediocrity, and doesn't seem to have any of the urgency of the rest of the record. Fortunately, it is the only disappointing moment of the album, and from here, it maintains and builds upon the standard set by the first four tracks.

For all Paramore's intuitive sense of melody and harmony, they had not yet managed to pen a ballad, either sweet or solemn, that matched the quality of their livelier tracks. They had fallen well short of the mark on *Riot!*, with 'When It Rains' and 'We Are Broken' feeling like the kind of pedestrian, sentimental exercises that you'd expect more from an air-headed pop crooner

– not a credible alternative band. But on *brand new eyes* they finally broke the duck with 'The Only Exception', and in spectacular style. It had originally been intended as a two-minute interlude, with just acoustic guitar and vocals, but the band had fallen so hard for it that it was developed into a four-minute song with full accompaniment. 'The Only Exception' is so daringly simple and plain, it ought to be dull. It's an acoustic love ballad in the tradition of almost every pop or rock band, ever. But its simplicity becomes its elegance and beauty, the plaintive and restrained melodies in the verse and chorus perfectly pitched to hit the listener where it hurts: their shrivelled, bitter hearts. Hayley resists the urge to display her vocal prowess, instead adopting a lilting style that is barely above a whisper. But it all builds to a fantastically moving climax, Hayley reaching into the upper register of her range as the drums kick in. You have to admire the honesty of the lyrics, too: the first verse surely concerns the disintegration of her parent's marriage, and it's not cloaked in weightless metaphor, but stated with a simple grace. Hayley sees it as the first love song she's ever written, and she was delighted with the way it turned out. "I like that I was able to express the fact that I have always been really afraid of love," she said. "But the excitement and the hope that it exists is still very evident in the lyrics."

'The Only Exception' marks a turning point in the record. The song is about emotional development from caution and cynicism to hope and love, and it also performs this function for the album as a whole. It is the point that the songs pivot around, from anger, frustration and conflict, to optimism, triumph, and joy. Thereafter 'Feeling Sorry' is the first of a trio of songs that head in the same direction. It is about casting off the burden of sympathy for people left behind and moving forward with your life. "It's frustrating whenever I see people with so much potential just throw away their dreams because they seem out of reach," said Hayley in *Alternative Press*. "It probably seems a bit like I'm talking down to anyone who isn't on tour or selling records. But it's not like that at all. It took a lot of sacrifice and years of touring and working our way from the ground up to get to this point." If you close your eyes and listen to the track, you can almost see Hayley stomping around the stage with annoyance. It's a raucous rock track shot through with grit and resolve. The simplicity of the pop-punk palm-muting in the verse is offset by the syncopated rhythms, and the chorus is big, brash and bloody-minded.

The final four songs of the record are its strongest third, though the tracks move in different directions. 'Looking Up' is a perfectly euphoric, joyous affair that is the exact counterbalance to 'Ignorance'. Hayley manages to sing about the joys of getting through the near-split, being in a band and living her dream without sounding smug, giving the song an irresistible charm that would get even the bitterest of cynics on their feet. For the first time she even sneaks in a little tongue-in-cheek wit at the expense of her critics: the world doesn't need another band, she observes in the breakdown, but what a waste it would've been if Paramore hadn't made it. On the strength of 'Looking Up', you can't help agreeing with her. The song was a result of Hayley and Taylor hassling Josh to come up with a feel-good song for the record. It was near the end of the recording process, and upon first hearing the music, Hayley knew that she had found the perfect platform to express her pride in Paramore. It's her favourite song on *brand new eyes*. 'Where The Lines Overlap' follows a similar path, and is the most indebted to pop-punk forefathers like The Descendents and The Get Up Kids. Josh accompanies Hayley in the verse over a simple, sunny buzz-saw guitar part, which is embellished with twinkling glockenspiel flourishes. There's not really a great deal to the song, but there doesn't need to be – it boasts one of the most triumphant and uplifting choruses on the album. In the breakdown Hayley indulges her passion for crowd interaction; she had previously spoke of how she loved hearing audiences shout the gang vocal parts of 'Born For This' back at her, and wanted to write another song that gave fans the chance to join in. 'Where The Lines Overlap' was obviously written with that intention. It is a brave gambit, but one that will surely be vindicated each time Paramore take to the road.

The final two songs of the album move away from the giddy joy of 'Looking Up' and 'Where The Lines Overlap'. 'Misguided Ghosts' is the second example of Paramore getting a ballad-type song right, even though it's about as far from their usual sound as they have ever ventured. The textured, finger-picked acoustic guitars tip the cap to nu-folk acts like Kings Of Convenience or José Gonzàlez, and it has a strong sense of Americana about it, which complements the road-tripping metaphor of the lyrics. It's just as successful as 'The Only Exception', Hayley's silk-soft vocals more gorgeous than ever before. The song was recorded live, Josh, Hayley and Taylor all performing in the same room simultaneously, rather than recording their parts individually; this gives the song a warm, rounded sound. Hayley describes it as the "red-headed stepchild" of the album: the music was written by Taylor on tour in England, while Paramore were still in the grip of inter-band turmoil. "I like it," said Hayley, "because it sort of

embodies every random, confusing emotion that I've ever had about living in this crazy world."

The final song on *brand new eyes* (aside from bonus track, 'Decode') is one of its real highlights, even though it nearly didn't make it on there. 'All I Wanted' again broaches territory that Paramore had not explored before; it has a lulling, sedate verse that explodes into an emphatically emotional chorus, borrowing from the swirling, wall-of-sound dynamics of bands like Deftones. While the verse has a restrained melancholy about it, Hayley's vocal in the chorus is one of the most impressive she has ever committed to record: a controlled but amazingly powerful wail (there is no other word to describe it) that is shot through with longing, sadness and raw emotion. It is a return to the dark period before the band had settled their differences, written during the long periods Hayley spent alone in her apartment feeling isolated and confused. For whatever reason, they initially felt it wouldn't be right for the album, but Hayley is glad they decided to put it on – "We would've been pissed right now if it wasn't there," she said. It would've been one of the finest songs never to make it to record.

brand new eyes is without a doubt Paramore's best album. Born of a period of intense strife and dissatisfaction for all of the band, it somehow manages to express all of the negative feelings they had in a coherent, satisfying and endlessly melodic end product. But what is most remarkable is the way you can hear the band battle through their problems during the album, moving from conflict and anger to reconciliation, joy and triumph.

Putting aside the story that it tells for a moment, *brand new eyes* is so good simply because it contains some of Paramore's best songs. On *Riot!* they had honed a distinct sound to the point of near-perfection, but the few attempts they made to expand on this central style represented that record's weakest moments. By contrast, on *brand new eyes*, the band push and pull their core sound in all manner of directions: furious, post-hardcore punk rock on 'Careful', beautifully crafted love balladry on 'The Only Exception' or slow-burning, epic alternative rock on 'All I Wanted' – but always guided by the band's irrefutable pop sensibilities. So in sharp contrast to the two previous albums, the instances when the band are at their most cautious is also when the third record is at its weakest, as on 'Turn it Off'. They had incubated their pop-punk-alternative-rock mongrel and then ran with it; to somewhere smarter, finer, and more powerful.

Paramore had never been darlings of the music media, but *brand new eyes* set about changing that. Critical acclaim had always largely alluded them, despite their huge popularity – though many journalists often included the cautious caveat that the band *could* be great given time to grow. *brand new eyes* convinced many people that Paramore were finally the band that many had hoped, but perhaps doubted, they were capable of becoming. *Kerrang!* had given the band plenty of coverage but only ever poor-to-average album reviews, but now they finally called an end to the stalemate. "In *brand new eyes* they have arguably delivered the most accomplished and affecting record of their career," Dan Slessor wrote, "that proves that Paramore are serious contenders for true rock greatness." He scored it four out of five K's. *NME* had also previously tended toward haughty disapproval when it came to Paramore, but they too thawed in the heat of *brand new eyes*. They were unsure of the album's slower moments, however, saying: "If you just so happen to be one of the best in the up-tempo pop-smattered emo-punk game, why bother slowing down?" *Alternative Press* had long been allies of the band, and they were unreserved in their praise of *brand new eyes*, awarding it 4.5 out of 5. "Aural proof that what doesn't kill you most certainly makes you stronger," the reviewer Scott Heisel wrote, "*eyes* astonishes from start to finish." In fact, critics were practically ready to retire their barbed tongues in exchange for praise of the album. *Absolutepunk.net* gave the album 82%; *Allmusic.com* called them a "stronger, leaner, and altogether more consistent band"; *Rock Sound* called it "by far their best album yet," and scored it nine out of ten: and *Drowned In Sound* called the band "irresistible," scoring the album eight out of ten. Where so many artists pretend to be completely disinterested in reviews, usually spouting some nonsense about the integrity of their art not needing approval from the press, Hayley was honest enough to admit she was delighted. The band who had long been fans' favourites had finally become the critics' darlings.

THE END OF THE BEGINNING

brand new eyes was released on September 29, 2009, to the best initial sales that Paramore had ever seen. It topped the charts in Australia, Ireland, New Zealand and the UK. In the USA it went straight in at Number 2 on the US *Billboard* 200, just behind Barbra Streisand's album *Love Is The Answer*. It was quickly announced as officially Paramore's most successful album to date.

When some bands drop off the radar to record an album, the whole music scene moves on without them and by the time they reappear, eager and ready to spring their new record on the world, no one really cares anymore. New bands and sounds may have emerged, and even within a few short months a band can go out of date. For other bands, their absence only heightens demand. When they leave, they create a hole that no other acts seem to be able to fill, and their reappearance is met with a near rabid enthusiasm. Paramore are the latter. A promo for 'Ignorance', directed by Honey, was released in August 2009, and shot to straight to the top of most alternative music channel's charts. The performance video is confrontational, claustrophobic and tense, Hayley shining a light bulb in the faces of her band mates as she sings. The single would be released in September, peaking at Number 4 in the UK singles chart, their highest position for a single to date.

A stadium tour around the US with the newly reformed No Doubt would also do much to put Paramore back in the public eye, but following the release of *brand new eyes*, they had their own headline tour to think about. It would be the first time they had hit the road as headliners in almost a year, and they weren't doing it by halves: it would take the band all over States through October and November, playing mainly mid-sized venues, and then to the UK via Finland, Sweden, Denmark, Germany, France and The Netherlands for some arena dates. The tour would end in spectacular style at the Wembley Arena in London, tickets for which sold out within a day of going on sale. But of course, it wouldn't be a headline Paramore tour if Hayley's voice didn't complicate matters, and on October 2, it was announced that a bout of laryngitis had forced her to go on voice rest for a week. Despite the visible disappointment of the band, the tour resumed on

October 9, and they got back the business of blowing away audiences again.

Amidst all of the success, it's easy to forget just how young Paramore still are at the time of writing. On this tour, Hayley will still be only 20; Jeremy remains the band's elder statesman at 25, and Zac will be playing to over 12,000 people at the tender age of nineteen. It's strange to think how far the band have come in their relatively brief lives on the planet. At fifteen they were excitedly signing record contracts and joining the Warped Tour, delighted to find a handful of people singing along. By eighteen they had released a hit follow-up to their debut that would take them across the planet on a world tour, playing hundreds of shows to hundreds of thousands of dedicated fans. They would go from actually living in one another's pockets to metaphorically lunging at one another's throats, and the band almost looked set to crumble before its average age reached 21. But something set Paramore apart and distinguished them from the crop of forgettable bands that find fame too fast, or not fast enough, and fall apart – the countless now-defunct acts that have crossed Paramore's path on those long days on the road. It is hard to pin down, an intangible connection that they have when they step in a room together, a little spark of uniqueness that you can see when you watch them onstage or hear when you listen to their best songs. It is something that has endured beyond the break-ups, line-up changes, fights and fatigue.

Just imagine where they'll be in ten years' time.